GW01220466

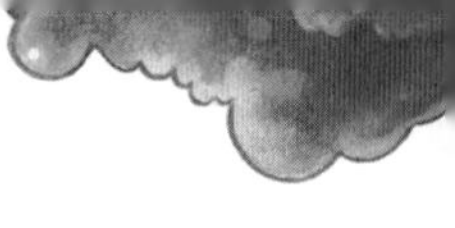

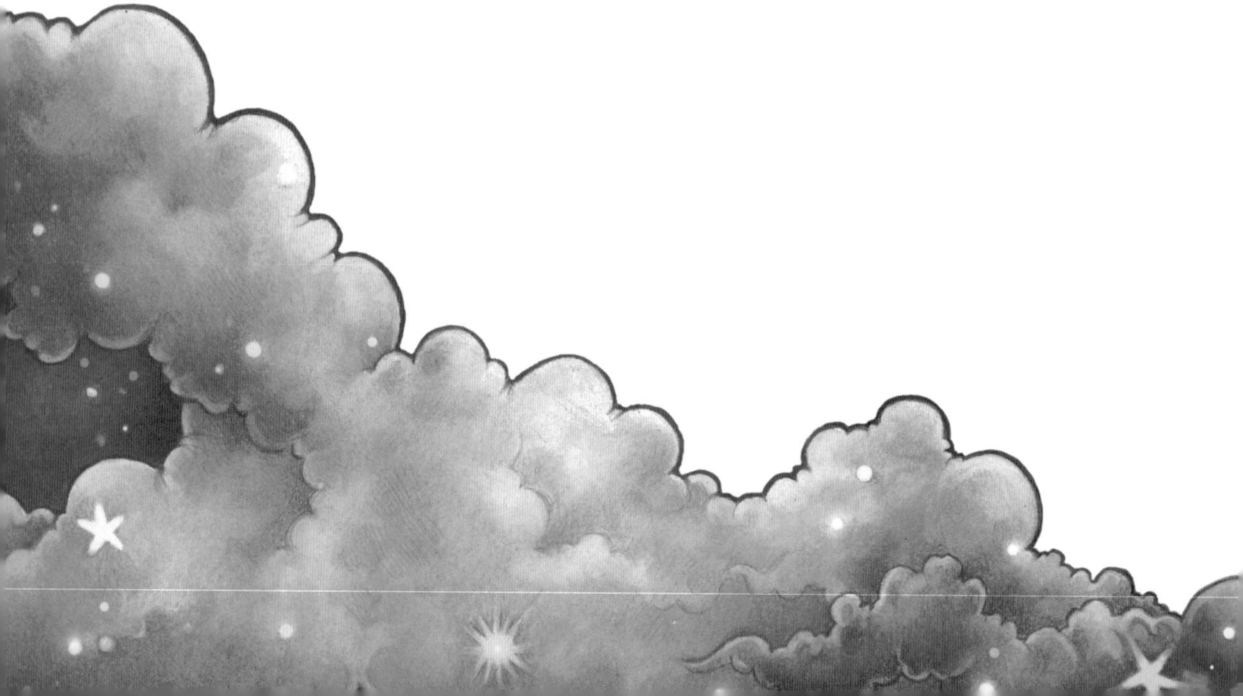

BRILLIANT!

28 Catholic Scientists, Mathematicians, and Supersmart People

SECOND EDITION

Written by David Michael Warren

Illustrated by Jaclyn Warren

Pauline
BOOKS & MEDIA
Boston

Library of Congress Control Number: 2021951123

CIP data is available.

ISBN 10: 0-8198-1252-8

ISBN 13: 978-0-8198-1252-0

Many manufacturers and sellers distinguish their products through the use of trademarks. Any trademarked designations that appear in this book are used in good faith but are not authorized by, associated with, or sponsored by the trademark owners.

Every effort has been made to trace copyright holders and to obtain their permission for the use of copyright material. The publisher apologizes for any errors or omissions in the above list and would be grateful if notified of any corrections that should be incorporated in future reprints or editions of this book.

Scripture texts in this work are taken from the *New American Bible, Revised Edition* © 2010, 1991, 1986, 1970 Confraternity of Christian Doctrine, Washington, D.C., and are used by permission of the copyright owner. All rights reserved. No part of the *New American Bible* may be reproduced in any form without permission in writing from the copyright owner.

Cover art by Jaclyn Warren

This cover has been designed using resources from Freepik.com: Premium golden & silver gradients swatches by Starline.

Content Advisor: Ryan Howard, M.S., M.Ed.

All rights reserved. No part of this book may be reproduced or transmitted in any form or by any means, electronic or mechanical, including photocopying, recording, or by any information storage and retrieval system, without permission in writing from the publisher.

"P" and PAULINE are registered trademarks of the Daughters of St. Paul.

Copyright © 2023, 2020, Jaclyn and David Michael Warren

Published by Pauline Books & Media, 50 Saint Pauls Avenue, Boston, MA 02130–3491

Printed in Korea

B SIPSKOGUNKYO 12-3110172 1252-8

www.pauline.org

Pauline Books & Media is the publishing house of the Daughters of St. Paul, an international congregation of women religious serving the Church with the communications media.

1 2 3 4 5 6 7 8 9 10   28 27 26 25 24 23

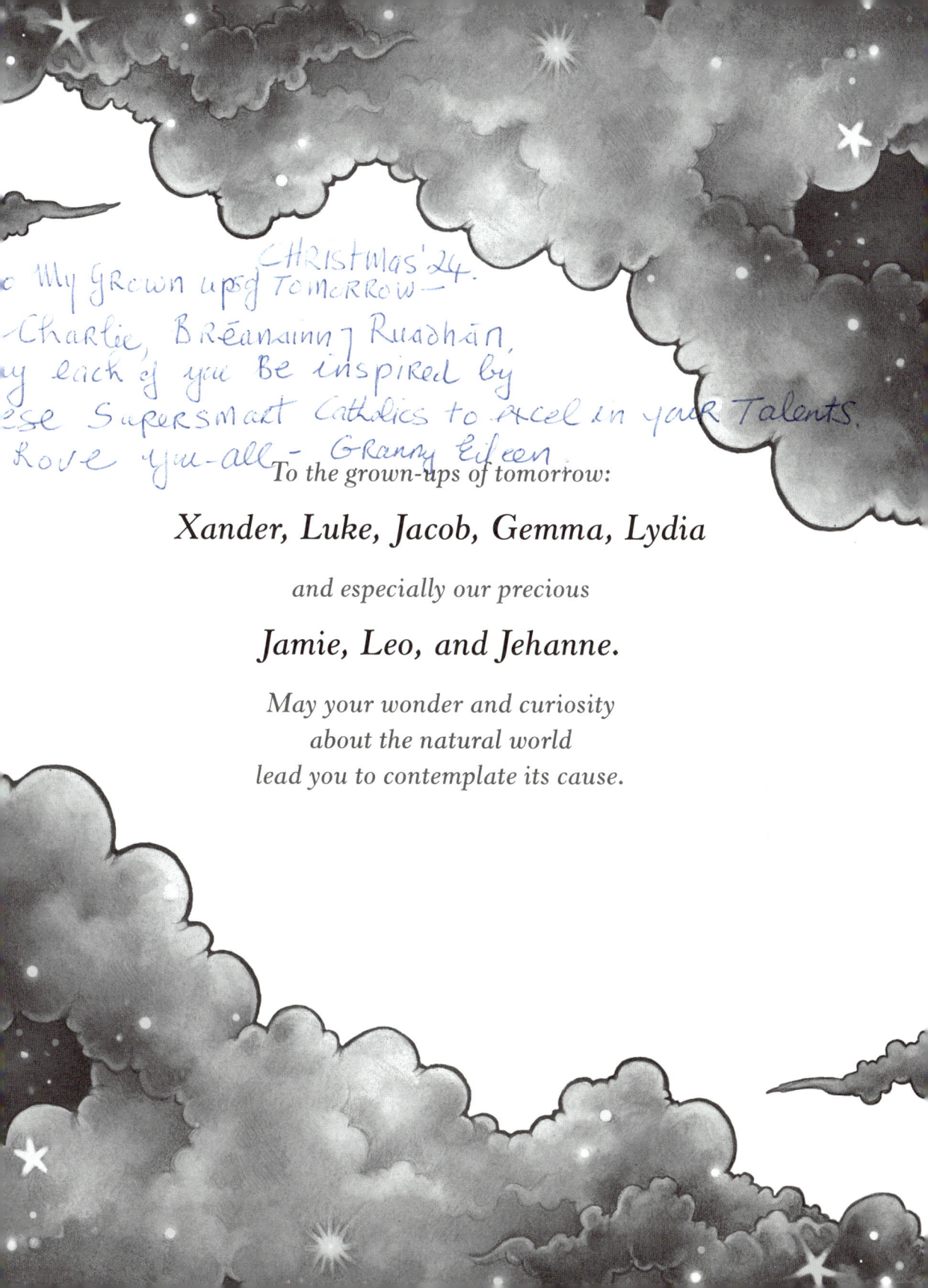

To my grown ups of tomorrow — Christmas '24.
Charlie, Bréanainn, Ruadhán,
May each of you be inspired by
these supersmart Catholics to excel in your talents.
Love you all — Granny Eileen.

To the grown-ups of tomorrow:

Xander, Luke, Jacob, Gemma, Lydia

and especially our precious

Jamie, Leo, and Jehanne.

May your wonder and curiosity
about the natural world
lead you to contemplate its cause.

Contents

Foreword x

Introduction 1

Saint Hildegard of Bingen: *Philosopher, Pharmacist, Playwright, Musician, Botanist, Doctor of the Church* 2

Saint Albert the Great: *Patron of Scientists and Philosophers* . . . 7

Nicolaus Copernicus: *Mathematician and Father of Modern Astronomy* 10

Father Christopher Clavius: *Mathematician* 15

Father Marin Mersenne: *Music Theorist, Mathematician, and Father of Acoustics* 18

Blessed Nicolas Steno: *Father of Modern Geology* 22

Giovanni Manzolini and Anna Morandi Manzolini: *Sculptors of Anatomy* 27

Laura Bassi: *First Female Professor of Physics* 31

Maria Agnesi: *Mathematician, Educator, and Humanitarian* 34

Louis Braille: *Educator, Inventor* 39

Father Angelo Secchi: *Astronomer, Pioneer of Astrophysics* 42

Father Léon Provancher: *Father of Natural History* 46

Louis Pasteur: *Founder of Microbiology* 50

Father Gregor Mendel: *Father of Modern Genetics* 54

Blessed José Gregorio Hernández: *Doctor of the Poor* 59

Adrian Atiman: *Survivor of Slavery, Missionary Doctor* 62

Father Henri Breuil: *Archaeologist and Natural Scientist* 67

Saint Giuseppe Moscati: *Medical Doctor and Chemist* 70

Father Georges Lemaître: *Father of the Big Bang Theory* 75

Sister Hilary Ross: *Researcher, Humanitarian* 78

Takashi Nagai: *Pioneer of Radiology, Survivor of the Atomic Bomb, Servant of God* 82

Sister Miriam Michael Stimson: *Chemist, DNA Pioneer* 87

Saint Gianna Beretta Molla: *Patron of Doctors, Mothers, and Unborn Children* 91

Sister Mary Kenneth Keller: *Pioneer in Computer Science* . . . 94

Jérôme Lejeune: *Pediatrician, Geneticist, Servant of God* 98

Pope Francis: *Environmentalist, Scientific Advocate* 103

Karin Öberg: *Astrochemist, Professor* 107

Glossary 110

Foreword

The book you are about to read is an amazing account of some of the most intelligent and gifted people who ever lived. Some are scientists or doctors. All of them cared about humanity and about nature. They made new and groundbreaking discoveries. They combined scientific genius with an eagerness to help others. In short, they were *Brilliant!* They were also Catholic. In fact, some of them are recognized by the Church as saints. They are examples for us not only because of their ingenuity, but also because of their faith, hope, and love.

If an invisible hand wiped their names from the pages of history, it would wipe out a great deal of our knowledge. We would not understand the age and formation of the Earth and the entire universe. We would not know the laws of plant and animal life, how stars form, or how our planet moves. Gone would be our modern calendar, our understanding of genetics, and many cures for horrible diseases. No one can turn back the clock and see what would have happened. Perhaps pioneers other than those you will read about in these pages would have made those discoveries. We will never know. But we do know that the contributions these twenty-five people made to human knowledge are irreplaceable. Their stories show us that intelligence and faith, science and holiness, do go together. In fact, they are made for each other.

In the pages to come, you will meet great Catholic scientists who believed in God. The work of Saint Albert the Great on plants and animals is known today as a groundbreaking masterpiece. The devout Frenchman Louis Pasteur founded microbiology and paved the way for modern medicine. The Belgian priest who saw Einstein's equations in a new way learned that the universe has been expanding from the moment of the Big Bang.

This book tells the truth. It is also illustrated with love and creativity. Each of the images tells a part of the story, capturing some unique aspect of that person. We can feel a bit of the awe, wonder, and joy of discovery that they must have felt as they set out to understand God's creation.

—*Chris Baglow, PhD, director of the Science and Religion Initiative of the McGrath Institute for Church Life at the University of Notre Dame*

Introduction

Have you heard these lies? You cannot be a true scientist and believe in God. Science proves that Christianity is outdated and mistaken. Certain parts of the Bible do not line up with modern science, so the whole thing is false and worthless. Not one of these statements is true.

A few years ago, my wife Jaclyn took her middle-school art class on a field trip to study mural paintings. One of her students saw a painting of Jesus and asked, "Why are we looking at paintings of God when he isn't even real?" Jaclyn responded with her own question, "Why do you think God isn't real?" His answer was short: "Because, science." This view is fairly common. Recent studies show that many people today—even many Christians—believe that religion and science are opposites. Sadly, people feel forced to choose between the two. Some even leave their faith behind because they think they have to "choose" science. But it doesn't have to be this way!

Students of science, math, philosophy, and religion are all searching for the same thing: truth! The same God who made the universe and all of creation also gave us logical minds so that we could use science and math. Scientific theories like the Big Bang and evolution don't threaten the Christian faith at all. Some of the greatest scientists, mathematicians, and inventors of all time believed in God and lived out their Catholicism. There were popes who encouraged and even paid for cutting-edge scientific research. You'll read about many of these supersmart innovators in this book.

Every biography and illustration in the following pages tells the story of a man or woman who was both devoted to God and influential in an intellectual field. Every one of them stands as proof that intelligence and faith can work together in a kind of harmony that leads to new discoveries that benefit the whole world. It's worth noting that there are many, many more brilliant Catholic people than this book can contain. I bet you are one of them! So, don't believe the lies. Don't settle for any faith that tells you to turn off your brain. Ask the biggest questions you can so that you may find and know the Truth!

Saint Hildegard of Bingen

Philosopher, Pharmacist, Playwright, Musician, Botanist, Doctor of the Church

(1098–September 17, 1179)

How would people react if you claimed to see things that they could not? What if you spent countless hours staring at plants or writing in your own language? Would people think you were crazy? Hildegard did all these things, but she was not crazy—she was a visionary woman of immense talent and religious insight. She became the **abbess** of two monasteries, composed music, and practiced the art of herbal medicine. She also wrote much about God and the Bible. Eventually, she became a world-famous scientist, saint, and a **Doctor of the Church**!

Hildegard was born into a noble German family. As a little girl, she had mystical visions about God. She sought spiritual guidance from Blessed Jutta, a Benedictine abbess. Hildegard's visions continued throughout her life. Jutta encouraged Hildegard to write about the visions and she personally educated Hildegard. The visions were recorded in detail and influenced Hildegard's ministry and teaching.

For as long as you live, your soul and body

together work

By the age of fifteen, Hildegard entered the monastery at Disibodenberg, Germany. There, she devoted her life to God. She prayed and worked together with other nuns. For Hildegard, this commitment meant using study, art, and other creative outlets as tools to grow closer to God. Hildegard studied the Psalms carefully. She wrote at least sixty-nine pieces of music based on them. Today, these songs make up one of the largest collections of music from the Middle Ages. Hildegard also wrote the first-known morality play, *Ordo Virtutum*. This kind of play teaches a valuable lesson. She developed a secret language, *lingua ignota*, with its own vocabulary and rules of grammar.

Hildegard was gifted in science. She knew medicine and **botany**. She studied herbs and their medicinal effects. Skilled at treating illnesses, Hildegard helped sick patients in the monastery's hospital. She wrote two long books about medicine: *Physica* and *Causae et Curae*. She also stressed the importance of spiritual healing.

Hildegard understood that both females and males have the same human dignity. Both are made in the image and likeness of God. This is different than what most people believed at the time. She also wrote about God's love, the relationship between soul and body, and the Eucharist.

By the time of her death in 1179, Hildegard had done several notable things. At the age of thirty-eight, she became the **prioress** of the Disibodenberg monastery. Later she founded a new monastery at Bingen. She stood up to an anti-Catholic emperor named Frederick Barbarossa. She also stood up to a group who taught false information about Christianity. Hildegard left behind a collection of mystical writings that are still valuable to read today. For her great scientific gifts, many Germans call Saint Hildegard the founder of scientific natural history. In 2012, Pope Benedict XVI canonized Hildegard a saint and declared her a Doctor of the Church. We celebrate her feast day on September 17.

> GOD – THE MOST TRUE MOST SWEET MOST POWERFUL FROM ETERNITY CAN BE KNOWN THROUGH HIS EFFECTS

Saint Albert the Great

Patron of Scientists and Philosophers

(c.1200–November 15, 1280)

Imagine if a single person wrote an encyclopedia's worth of knowledge, discovered a new chemical, translated Greek philosophers, and won almost every argument he ever had. It would be fair to think that this person was a natural-born genius or had some secret explanation for his amazing intellect. Well, Saint Albert the Great (also known as Albertus Magnus) was not born a genius. He worked very hard before he earned the nickname "Teacher of All Things." Albert did have an explanation for his intellectual breakthroughs other than hard work: the Virgin Mary.

Albert was born in Germany and studied at the University of Padua. In 1223, Blessed Jordan of Saxony suggested that Albert join the Dominicans. Albert did so, but his smart peers made him feel overwhelmed. He prayed to the Blessed Virgin for help. He asked for knowledge, firm faith, and speech that would lead people to Christ. His prayer was answered. Albert grew in knowledge and boldness. After he completed his studies, he became a respected teacher in Germany. He commented on the works of Aristotle, an ancient Greek philosopher (384–322 BC), and taught people how to understand them.

Albert gave speeches and engaged in debates. He met teachers who taught things against the Catholic faith and he faced attacks from intellectual people. Albert worried that his faith would be shaken. Again, he turned to Mary in prayer. Mary told him that he would not lose his faith. She also said that he would be given a sign when his death was near. He would know that his life was coming to an end when he lost his gift for public argument. His confidence was restored.

Albert was also very interested in the natural sciences. He wrote scientific papers about the stars, the Earth, plants, and animals. He conducted experiments with **silver nitrate** and other chemicals. Albert was the first to discover the dangerous chemical known as **arsenic**. He was intrigued by falcons and wrote about them at length in a large book about animals. In addition, Albert spent long hours studying bees and their behavior. His writings, which fill up thirty-eight volumes, are like an encyclopedia of information. His work is still impressive eight hundred years later.

In 1245, Albert became the first German Dominican to hold the title of Master of Theology. He became a professor at the University of Paris. He taught many scholars, including the young Saint Thomas Aquinas, who became one of the Church's greatest theologians. Aquinas was often teased in class because he didn't say much and had a large body-build, but Albert saw something special in him. Albert said, "You call this young man a dumb ox, but I tell you, one day this ox will bellow so loud that it will resound throughout the whole world!" Of course, Aquinas became a wonderful teacher and fellow saint!

Albert spent countless hours in adoration before the Blessed Sacrament. His friends often found him praying and thinking deeply near the Eucharist. Albert became a bishop in 1260. He only traveled by foot and refused to ride a horse. He earned a second nickname,

"Bishop Boots." Being a bishop did not last long. Albert convinced the pope that he could better serve the Church as a problem-solver. He spent his time helping people sort out their differences.

In the late 1270s, Albert recognized the sign of his approaching death that Mary had told him about years before: he lost a public debate. He understood that this meant he could return to God like a simple child. He left these words for his students, "Strive with all your powers . . . that you may attain the knowledge of [Jesus'] Divinity through the wounds of His Sacred Humanity." He passed away in a Dominican friary in Cologne on November 15, 1280.

Today, interest in Albert remains strong. Readers can find references to him in Dante Alighieri's *Divine Comedy*, Mary Shelley's *Frankenstein*, and even J. K. Rowling's *Harry Potter* series. Albert was named a saint in 1931 and given the title Doctor of the Church. Many schools are named after him today.

Nicolaus Copernicus

Mathematician and Father of Modern Astronomy
(February 19, 1473–May 24, 1543)

For ages, people have looked up at the stars hoping to understand their place in the universe. When Nicolaus Copernicus looked, he saw the same stars, but in a new way. His insight challenged what people understood and forever changed the study of astronomy.

Nicolaus was born the youngest of four children in Toruń, Poland, on February 19, 1473. All the members of his family were well-educated Catholics. When Nicolaus was eleven, his father passed away. He went to live with his devout Catholic uncle, Lucas Watzenrode.

Nicolaus entered the University of Kraków where he studied **astronomy**, math, and **philosophy**. He also spoke many languages including German, Polish, Greek, Italian, and Latin. Before his graduation, Nicolaus left school at the urging of his uncle, who had become a bishop and wanted Nicolaus to serve the Church. Nicolaus learned a good deal about medicine and helped those who were sick. He also assisted his uncle as a secretary, handling many Church matters. Nicolaus studied Church Law in Italy, but his true passion was the stars. He believed that studying the universe would deepen his admiration of God. Some accounts suggest that Nicolaus became a priest, but actually, he joined the Third Order of Saint Dominic to live out his Christian faith in the secular world.

While Nicolaus was in Italy, he studied with the astronomer Domenico Maria Novara. Nicolaus learned about the geocentric

Hypothesis Copernicana

THE MACHINERY OF THE UNIVERSE HAS BEEN BUILT BY A SUPREMELY GOOD AND ORDERLY CREATOR

model of the universe. This model placed the Earth at the center of the **solar system**. At that time people believed in the geocentric model because it matched what they saw. For one thing, the Earth seemed stationary when a person looked at the changing sky. Although the sun appeared to rise and set, the Earth did not seem to move at all. Moreover, great thinkers, such as Aristotle (384–322 BC) and Ptolemy (c. 100–c. 170 AD), all believed in this model too.

After a while, Copernicus started to see problems with the geocentric model. First, it did not make sense with the calendar of his time, the **Julian calendar**. The geocentric model called for a calendar year that was about eleven minutes too short. This might not seem like much time, but it added up over the years. Second, Copernicus noticed the planets would be brighter and bigger or dimmer and smaller depending on what night it was. If the planets went around the Earth in perfect circles—as the geocentric model claimed—they would always look the same.

Copernicus wanted to develop a model of the solar system that could make sense of these issues. He had the new idea that our solar system was **heliocentric**, not geocentric. This meant that the sun, not the Earth, was the center of our solar system! Suddenly, the universe made sense!

Nicolaus knew that people would challenge his ideas. Nevertheless, he believed that it was his duty to seek the truth in all things. For thirty-six years he worked hard on his model and did a lot of research. Just before his death at the age of seventy, Nicolaus published his work in a book titled *On the Revolutions of the Celestial Spheres*.

There was some opposition to Nicolaus' idea about the Earth moving, but not as much as some people claim. Some people think that the Catholic Church banned his work. Others think that people tortured Copernicus for his idea. Neither account is true. Copernicus received formal permission from the Church before he published his work. He even wrote the dedication of the book to Pope Paul III. Catholic universities read and taught Copernicus' work shortly after its publication. The Catholic Church never banned Copernicus' book. The Church only paused its publication for four years, between 1616 and 1620. Why? The Church wanted to closely examine the book's claims before approving it. So, what was the controversy?

Some Christians read every part of the Bible as scientific fact. These Christians pointed to Psalm 93:1, which says: "The world will surely stand in place, never to be moved." They believed that this piece of poetry was scientifically factual. They could not understand the idea that the Earth *moved* around the sun. Sadly, many people did not accept Copernicus' way of seeing the universe. The people who could not see the truth of his claim called him a fool for his beliefs. Thankfully, Copernicus trusted God and his ideas. He changed the world by remaining faithful to both.

Eventually, scientists began to prove Copernicus' ideas were accurate and they became widely accepted. Over time, scientists were able to build upon his ideas as they discovered that the universe was bigger than our solar system! Nicolaus Copernicus was a faithful Catholic whose work shaped our understanding of our place in the universe. Today, we call him the father of modern astronomy. We also see his work as the beginning of the scientific revolution.

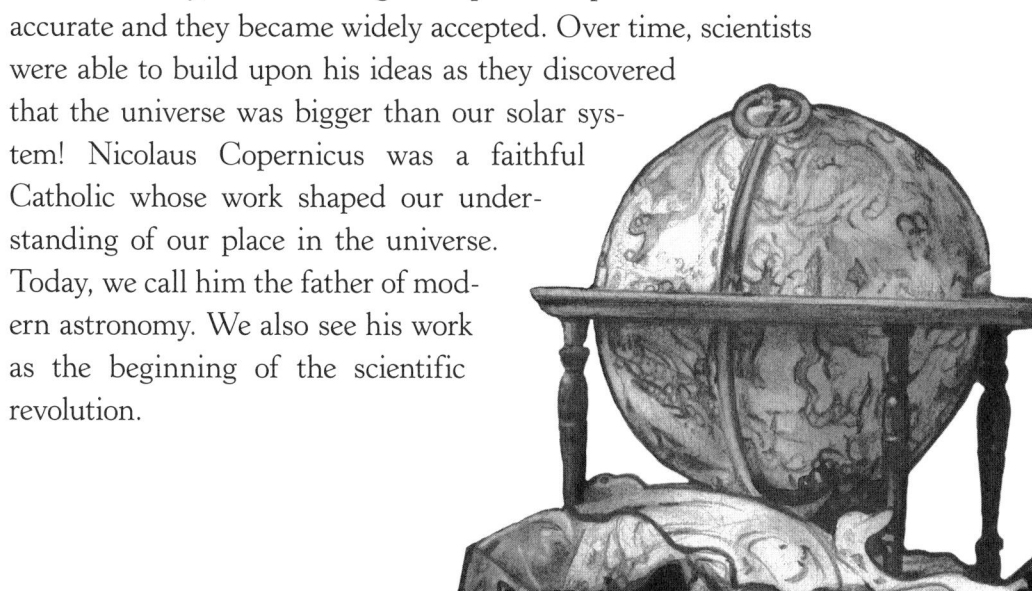

Teach us to count our days aright • XI
that we may gain wisdom of heart
AUGUSTUS
SEPTEMBER
OCTOBER
NOVEMBER
DECEMBER

Father Christopher Clavius

Mathematician
(March 25, 1538–February 6, 1612)

Some problems take a very long time to solve. A problem with the calendar puzzled the world for over fifteen hundred years! Between 46 BC and 1582 AD, the world used the Julian calendar to keep track of the days. Unfortunately, the Julian calendar had a flaw. It did not line up with the movement of the sun, stars, or moon. This was a problem since the lunar cycle was used to choose the dates of some holy days, such as Easter. Over many years, some holy days drifted into different months. Had this been left uncorrected, we might celebrate Easter in October! Thankfully, a Catholic priest named Christopher Clavius found the solution.

Clavius was born in Bavaria, joined the Jesuit order in 1555, and was sent to study at a university in Portugal. Christopher learned all he could about Scripture, the work of Aristotle, and physics. One day in 1560, Christopher saw something amazing. The sky swiftly grew dark and some birds fell to the ground. The sun disappeared in an **eclipse**! The amazing sight impressed and interested him. He wondered about what he had seen, so he decided to study the stars and the planets.

Christopher went to the Jesuit College in Rome and learned astronomy, math, and theology. He became a priest in 1564 and taught in Rome. Christopher wrote books about algebra and was the first German to use the decimal point. Before long, he was an expert in astronomy. Pope Gregory XIII asked him to lead a team of mathematicians to solve the calendar problem.

Father Christopher and his team came up with a solution that shortened the length of each year by ten minutes. This may not seem like a very big change, but it helped the calendar to line up with the **tropical year**—the actual length of time it takes for the Earth to circle the sun. They also came up with special rules for leap years. These changes helped the calendar stay lined up with the lunar cycle and prevented the drift of holy days. The new calendar was named the Gregorian calendar and was adopted in 1582. Ten days had to be dropped in order to correct the time lapse that had occurred during the years when the Julian calendar was used. The Gregorian calendar is the same calendar we use today.

Father Christopher desired to share his beliefs with others. He taught that math was important because it helps us understand nature and creation. When we learn about nature and creation, we also learn about the Creator. Therefore, Father Christopher said that doing math should be seen as an exercise of faith.

Solving the calendar problem was his most well-known feat, but it was not his only one. He wrote a book that explains advanced math, and he designed tools that could measure the tiny fractions of an angle. Father Christopher also wrote sacred music using mathematical formulas. He even provided mathematical proof for some of Galileo's discoveries. He also developed a set of math lessons to be taught in schools. Missionaries took these lessons and taught them around the world.

After Father Christopher died, scientists named a crater on the moon and an asteroid after him.

And the ear and en- Mu- sic is made to charm the spir- it a- ble us to

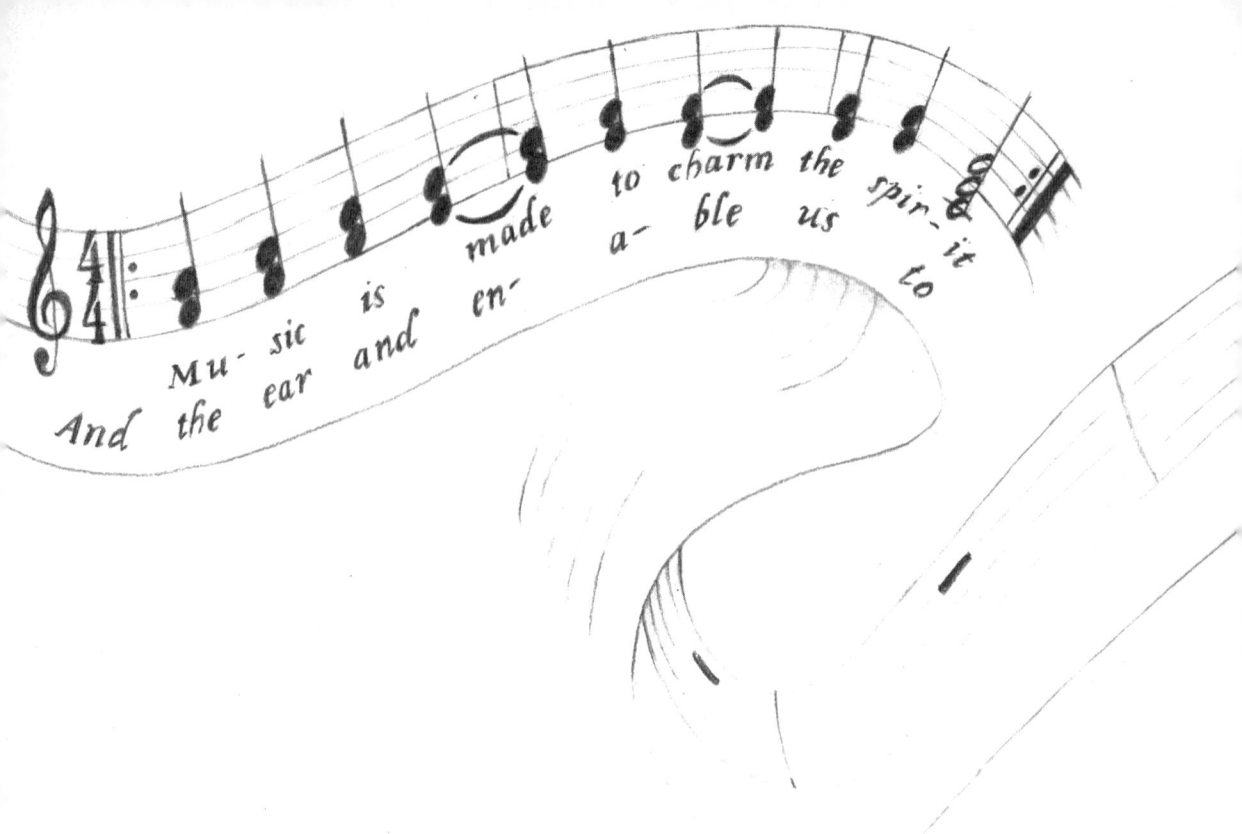

Father Marin Mersenne

Music Theorist, Mathematician, and Father of Acoustics
(September 8, 1588–September 1, 1648)

$$f_0 = \frac{\nu}{\lambda} = \frac{1}{2L}\sqrt{\frac{F}{\mu}}.$$

The equation above is about stringed musical instruments. It explains how string length, movement, mass, and force make up **pitch**. Many great thinkers have been stumped by the science behind **harmonics**. Fortunately, a Catholic priest named Father Marin Mersenne came up with the equation above. He improved the building and playing of stringed instruments. He also thought about **prime numbers** and helped the world's most brilliant thinkers work together.

Live with a li-ttle sweet-ness amidst all the bit-ter-ness we en-count-er

Marin was born in France. His parents wanted to educate their son and train him in the Catholic faith. Young Marin took grammar classes, but his family could not afford more education than that. The Jesuits opened a school that accepted even those who could not afford to pay for it. Marin was welcomed at the school and excelled there.

After graduation, Marin moved to Paris to keep learning. While on his way there, he stopped at a monastery belonging to the Order of Minims. These monks were devoted to poverty, learning, and obedience. The monks' behavior impressed Marin. He began to think about joining them one day.

First, Marin attended the Royal College in Paris. He studied Hebrew, theology, and philosophy. Marin graduated in 1611 and returned to the Minim Monastery where he joined the order and was ordained in 1612. At the age of twenty-six, Marin became the leader of a monastery in Paris where he would live and study for the rest of his life. He wrote important books about reason, the spiritual life, and science. The greatest thinkers in Europe noticed Marin's writings and visited him in his monastery.

Some of his guests were astronomer Pierre Gassendi, philosopher René Descartes, and mathematician Blaise Pascal. Marin saw the value of teamwork and formed a network of scientists from related fields. He translated and mailed letters to scientists from all over the world. This network was the precursor to the Paris Academy and had about 140 members. It was made up of astronomers, mathematicians, and philosophers such as Galileo Galilei. Over time, the group became known as the Academy of Sciences in Paris and inspired the Royal Society in London.

Some people say that the 1600s was a time when the Catholic Church was against science. But the truth is that a Catholic priest leading a monastery was at the center of the scientific world. He helped to improve scientific research by bringing together many minds. He studied a newly found curve called the **cycloid**. Marin also came up with the formula for expressing prime numbers. Meanwhile he continued to serve in his priestly ministry.

In addition, Marin played music and studied the science of sound. In 1636, he wrote a book about music theory, *The Universal Harmony*. The book teaches how to build stringed instruments and explains Mersenne's Laws for pitch. Even today guitars, violins, and other stringed instruments are made according to Mersenne's Laws.

Marin died from complications due to a lung problem. As he had requested, his body was donated to science so it could be studied. Today, Marin is best remembered as a music theorist and the namesake of Mersenne Prime Numbers.

Blessed Nicolas Steno

Father of Modern Geology
(January 11, 1638–December 5, 1686)

Nicolas Steno (also known as Niels Stensen) was born to a Lutheran family in Denmark. At age three, he became seriously ill. At age six, his father passed away. Then an outbreak of the plague claimed the lives of two hundred forty students at his school. By the time Nicolas was eighteen, the events of his life caused him to question his Christian faith.

As a young man, Nicolas studied medicine. He was surrounded by people of all different beliefs and religions. Even the Christians he encountered had different ideas and beliefs about what was true. In response, he claimed to only believe in the things he could measure and examine himself.

> Though my flesh and my heart fail, God is the rock of my heart, my portion forever.

In 1662, Nicolas dissected a human heart. He was overwhelmed by the complexity of the muscle. The experience renewed his belief in an intelligent Creator. He believed in God, but he still wondered if the beliefs of Christians were true.

Nicolas studied many religions and felt that most of them were man-made. However, something was different about the Catholic Church. He was amazed that Catholics could trace their foundation back to Jesus' time. He said, "Either every religion is equally good, or only the Catholic religion is true." The puzzle made him restless for the next several years as he traveled through France and Italy advancing his scientific career.

Nicolas earned fame as an **anatomist** and became a university professor. He made discoveries in science that challenged the common thinking of his time. In 1666, the Grand Duke of Tuscany invited him to live in his palace and serve as a personal doctor and researcher. This chance gave Nicolas fame, wealth, and comfort.

One day, two fishermen caught a great white shark and Nicolas was asked to study it. It was so large that its liver alone weighed 220 pounds! He was amazed by the shark's teeth. They looked just like small objects called "tongue stones" that were found in rocks throughout Europe.

For many years, people had believed that "tongue stones" fell from the sky during lunar eclipses, even though there was no evidence for that. Nicolas realized that the "tongue stones" found in rock layers were actually sharks' teeth. He figured out that many dry areas of land must have once been covered by ocean. He came up with the **Principle of Superposition** to explain the odd finding. This idea states that **strata**, or layers of the Earth, are stacked on top of one another over very long periods of time. He said that when rocks pile up in layers, the oldest layers are at the bottom and the newest layers are on the top. Sometimes, movements in the Earth could cause these old layers to be moved closer to the surface. This principle explained how sharks' teeth ended up in stones and it proved the myth of "tongue stones" to be false. Nicolas' idea also made scientists question the age of the Earth. People started to think that the Earth's many layers of strata meant the Earth was much older than just a few thousand years, as many people believed. Because of his work in this area, Nicolas is considered the father of modern geology.

Nicolas went to Rome to meet Pope Alexander VII. On his way back from the meeting, he saw a procession with the Holy Eucharist on the feast of Corpus Christi. He was impressed that Catholics could see the host as the Body of Christ. All of his unanswered questions about Catholicism came back to him. In a letter to a friend, Nicolas wrote, "Either that host is nothing but a piece of bread, and those who are showing it such honor are bewitched, or else it really is the body of Jesus Christ—and in that case, why do I not [honor] it as well?"

Nicolas befriended a Poor Clare nun, a few clergymen, and a noblewoman to discuss the Catholic faith. His new friends shared logical reasons to become Catholic. Nicolas pondered what they said. He thought that God was speaking to him through his friends.

He realized that his mind had been so focused on material things, that he could not hear the voice of God. He came to understand that there are some truths that science cannot measure. Nicolas decided to become a Catholic and entered the Church on November 2, 1667. In 1675, he became a priest. Two years later, he became a bishop. Nicolas gave all of his wealth away. He chose to be poor and he often fasted. He wanted to share his greatest personal discovery, the Catholic faith, with others. He wrote sixteen books on the subject.

Toward the end of 1686, Steno became ill and prepared for his death. He blessed Catholics and Protestants on his deathbed and prayed for their unity. Pope Saint John Paul II beatified Nicolas Steno in 1988.

Touch provides more precise ideas than sight can give

Giovanni Manzolini and Anna Morandi Manzolini

Sculptors of Anatomy

(Giovanni: **1700–1755**)
(Anna: **January 21, 1714–July 9, 1774**)

Doctors and surgeons are experts in the field of **anatomy**—the study of the human body and its organs. Medical students must learn about body parts like bones, organs, tissues, and muscles. That is why they dissect, or cut open, and study dead bodies. What if medical students were not allowed to do this training? In the 1700s, Italian laws made dissecting dead bodies rather difficult. As a result, fewer people were able to become doctors. With fewer doctors, diseases quickly spread and treatments became rare. Italy faced a health crisis. Thankfully the Manzolinis, a husband and wife team, used their artistic skills to teach anatomy. Their work enabled many people to become doctors and eventually save many lives.

Giovanni Manzolini was a skilled artist who made realistic wax sculptures. His wife, Anna, knew a great deal about anatomy. The couple knew that realistic sculptures of the inside of human bodies could be very useful for training doctors. Before they could make the sculptures life-like, they would need access to bodies.

Around this time, Pope Benedict XIV helped people understand that there should be unity between faith and science. He explained that people could choose to leave their bodies for scientists to do research. He worked with Italian lawmakers to make it possible for scientists to access and study bodies. Then the Pope asked Catholics to donate bodies for study.

Giovanni and Anna decided to change their home into a lab and school of anatomy. They would make the best wax sculptures the world had ever seen right in their living room! The couple worked together and carefully cut open bodies. They used plaster and colored wax to sculpt body parts. People who saw their sculptures were amazed! Many people sometimes could not see the difference between the wax sculpture and the real thing. Museums, universities, and doctors hired the couple to make more sculptures. The Manzolinis sculpted the tiny parts of the inner ear, the reproductive system, bones, muscles, kidneys, and more.

Pope Benedict XIV also asked women to consider studying science. That was unusual at the time. Sometimes audiences showed up at the Manzolini home to watch the pair in action. The people were surprised when Anna cut open bodies and taught anatomy by herself. The Pope became the couple's greatest supporter. He hired the couple to make sculptures for the Academy of Sciences of Bologna Institute. Catherine the Great and other world leaders became fans of the work as well.

In 1755, Giovanni became ill and died. Anna was left with two boys to raise. Hard times fell upon her. Anna ran out of money and had to make arrangements for one of her children to be raised by someone else. It would have been understandable for Anna to hang up her tools and quit. The Pope knew that her scientific work was valuable, so he asked her to teach anatomy at the University of Bologna. She accepted and became a distinguished teacher. She was also honored by government officials, invited to teach in Moscow, and became a member of the British Royal Society.

During their careers Giovanni and Anna Manzolini cut open and studied over a thousand bodies. They taught many students valuable scientific knowledge about the human body. Today, Anna is remembered as a leader for female scientists. The couple's work can still be seen in the Academy of Sciences of Bologna Institute.

she opens her mouth

Laura Bassi

First Female Professor of Physics
(October 31, 1711–February 20, 1778)

The City of Bologna was buzzing on April 17, 1732. A silversmith made a special coin to remember the day. A poet wrote verses about what was happening. Royal people, lawmakers, and thousands of jubilant citizens flooded the streets. What was the occasion?

The city gathered to watch a brilliant twenty-year-old woman named Laura Bassi prove that she was smart enough to be a professor. If she could correctly answer tough questions about what she had learned, then she would earn a doctorate in physics. This would allow her to become the world's first female professor of physics at the university level.

When Laura was born, people thought that men were smarter than women. Women were limited to learning only basic reading and home skills, while men were taught advanced science and math. No woman had ever been a university professor of physics.

Fortunately, Laura's father knew she was just as smart as boys. He decided to make sure that she would receive an advanced education. He wanted her to learn Latin, so he asked a cousin, a priest named Father Stegani, to teach the language to Laura. He agreed and began to teach Laura when she was only five. She picked it up right away.

When Laura was thirteen, her father hired a university professor to tutor her in physics and logic. Adults who met Laura were shocked by her knowledge. People said she was a prodigy.

Philosophers, doctors, and other important people in Bologna showed up at Laura's home to meet her. They would ask her to speak in French and Greek, and were amazed at how well she did. Her home became a gathering place for debates and lessons. Archbishop Lambertini (later Pope Benedict XIV) saw Laura as proof that women could learn advanced science and math. He wanted her to keep learning, so he helped pay to further her education.

Laura became the first female member of the Academy of Sciences of Bologna Institute. Many of the members were upset that a woman was joining them. They said that Laura's membership was only honorary. They did not expect her to actually attend or speak up at meetings. But Laura did just that.

City officials decided to give Laura a chance to earn her doctorate and become a professor. Laura faced a lot of pressure to accomplish this difficult task. She would have to prove that a woman was intelligent enough to teach at a university. If she failed, careers for women might remain limited. Laura's test wasn't just about her. It was about all women.

When April 17, 1732 arrived, Laura stood before thousands of onlookers. She defended her years of research and study. She scientifically explained the properties of water. She discussed physics, reason, and the nature of God. She spoke in Latin and answered complex questions. When she finally finished, the crowd erupted with cheers and applause. On May 12, Laura was given a silver wreath, a fine ring, and a doctorate degree.

Laura became a physics professor. She continued to study the work of Sir Isaac Newton and was given access to a special library at the Vatican.

In 1738, Laura married a professor named Giovanni Veratti. Many people were concerned that marriage would distract Laura from her studies and teaching. However, they were wrong. Giovanni and Laura looked forward to having a family. Laura and Giovanni had many children, but they still found time to conduct experiments. They made discoveries about electricity, physics, and magnetism.

In 1745, Laura was the only woman invited to join a respected group of scientists gathered together by the pope. By the end of her career, she was well-respected and a professor of the highest rank at the University of Bologna. She also taught at a seminary until her unexpected death from a heart problem.

Laura Bassi defied expectations. She is remembered as a scientist, teacher, and trailblazer for women. Those who knew her best said she was a strong Catholic, a lover of poetry, and a caregiver to the poor. Her legacy is honored by a marble statue in the Bologna Institute of Science, the name of a high school in Italy, and the name of a crater on the planet Venus. She paved the way for women working in higher education all around the world.

Maria Agnesi

Mathematician, Educator, and Humanitarian
(May 16, 1718–January 9, 1799)

Calculus is a type of math that helps us understand and predict changes. It is useful for scientists, doctors, and engineers. However, calculus can be hard to understand. Many people who studied calculus in the 1700s struggled and gave up. Thankfully, Maria Agnesi understood it well. After explaining calculus to her younger siblings, she found a way to make it understandable to the world.

Maria was born in Milan, Italy. She was part of a wealthy Catholic family and was the oldest of twenty-one siblings and half-siblings. Her father made sure that each of his children got the best education possible. Maria loved studying languages and had a deep desire to serve others.

By age five, Maria spoke both Italian and French. Her father invited public figures to his home to hear his daughter speak. When she was only nine, Maria gave a speech in Latin. She explained why

> **THE VIRTUES of CHRIST** shine like stupendous stars and elevate the human mind to contemplate them in marvel, and the heart to imitate them with love.

girls should be well-educated. By eleven, Maria spoke seven languages including Greek, Spanish, Hebrew, and German.

Maria's father was proud of her and wanted to display her gift of knowledge to others. Maria, however, grew tired of putting on shows. She was shy and did not want to be famous. In fact, she asked her father if she could become a nun to serve the poor. Her father made a deal with her: if she would study advanced mathematics, he would let her serve the poor as much as time allowed her to do so.

Maria mastered algebra, geometry, and ballistics—the study of projectiles or objects that are moving through the air. She wrote commentaries about natural philosophy and the geometry of cones. Soon Maria was working with experts and writing about many areas of mathematics.

Maria also wanted to share her knowledge with her younger siblings. She tried to make complicated ideas simple. Maria wrote clear explanations about calculus and other branches of mathematics. By the time she had finished, she realized that she had written a book that could be helpful for many people.

The book was printed and reached a wide audience. People who struggled with calculus suddenly found it understandable. World leaders sent Maria gifts to thank her for her wonderful book. Maria dedicated her book to Empress Maria Theresa of Austria, who sent her a diamond ring. Pope Benedict XIV, who supported teachers like Giovanni and Anna Manzolini and Laura Bassi, sent her a gold rosary and a medal.

By the time Maria was in her early thirties, she was a respected math expert. In 1750, the University of Bologna offered her the head position in its math and physics program. Even though this was a tremendous opportunity, Maria never actually served in this position.

Two years later, in 1752, Maria's father passed away. Maria inherited a large sum of money, which made her very wealthy. But

Maria did not want money. She wanted to serve God and other people. She gave her inheritance to the poor.

Maria cared for those in need over the next several years. She taught young girls and looked after the elderly. In 1771, she was asked to be the director of the women's section of a nursing home. Maria lived and worked with nuns who ran the home. Together they cared for the sick, elderly, and mentally ill.

Maria passed away at the age of 80. Although she had come from a very rich family, she died poor and was buried in a common grave. Her choice to be poor baffled some people. Why would anyone choose to be poor? Maria's own words help us to understand. "Man always acts to achieve goals; the goal of the Christian is the glory of God . . . I hope my studies have brought glory to God [and that they] were useful to others . . . because that was my father's will."

Scientists named an asteroid and a crater on the planet Venus after Maria Agnesi. Mathematicians know her as the namesake for a curve used in calculus.

BLESSED are the pure of HEART

Louis Braille

Educator, Inventor

(January 4, 1809–January 6, 1852)

Have you noticed tiny bumps on elevator buttons? How about on bank machines and public signs? What are they? Those bumps are a special form of writing for people who cannot see well or at all. They allow the blind to read with their fingers. This form of writing would not exist without a Catholic inventor named Louis Braille.

Louis was born in a small town near Paris, France. His father was a leather worker who used a sharp, pointed tool called an awl to make holes in the leather. As a toddler, Louis sat in his father's shop and watched him work. When he was only three, Louis picked up his father's awl and accidentally injured his own eye. He was rushed to a doctor, but little could be done to save the eye. Then, a painful infection spread from his injured eye to the other. Soon after, Louis' world became dark. He never saw again.

Louis' parents loved him and wanted him to lead a normal life. His father made him walking canes to help him get around. Neighbors said that Louis was a smart boy with tenacity—the ability to keep going, even when things are tough. When he was six, Louis met a priest named Father Palluy. The priest taught Louis lessons that other boys were learning in school. He also taught Louis about God and helped him get into the Royal Institution for Blind Youth in Paris.

Louis' father missed him while he was away at school, so he found a way to help him write letters. He made Louis an alphabet out of thick leather strips. Louis arranged and traced these strips on paper so that he could write home. But the method of reading and writing by tracing the shape of each letter was hard and took a long time. Louis wished for an easier, faster way for blind people to read and write.

When he was a teenager, Louis invented his own method for blind people to "see" the alphabet on paper. Now known as Braille, it was inspired by a system created by Charles Barbier. Unlike Barbier's system, Braille letters could be read with a single touch. The twenty-six letters of the alphabet were represented using raised dots on paper. Each letter was made up of a unique combination of up to six dots. This new way of making letters could be quickly felt and "read" by the finger. Louis used an awl, the same tool that had blinded him, to impress these dots on a page. When he was fifteen, he shared his invention with others. Blind readers said that Louis' system was much faster to read than the old method of tracing the shape of every letter.

Louis did more than just help blind people to read and write letters. He helped them read music too! Louis played the cello or the organ every Sunday at a church in Paris. He wanted blind people to be able to read music as easily as they could read Braille. He adjusted his method to include symbols for math and musical notation.

At twenty-four, Louis shared the same gift of empowerment that Father Palluy had once given to him. He worked with blind children and became a teacher of math and history. His students felt that Louis was a very kind teacher. He spent little money on himself so that he could purchase instructional materials for students. Sometimes he would pay a poor student to copy a book in Braille. After the student was done copying it, he would give the book away to someone else who would like to read it. Students who could not afford books borrowed money from Louis and agreed that they would one day pay him back.

When he was in his twenties, Louis developed tuberculosis. For many years his health slowly declined, and by the time he was forty-three, Louis became very ill. He received Holy Communion and sensed that he would not live much longer. He told a friend, "God was pleased to hold before my eyes the dazzling splendors of eternal hope. After that, doesn't it seem that nothing more could keep me bound to the Earth?"

After he died, Louis' friends discovered a box that he had left behind. It had instructions written on it saying that the box should remain shut and be burned. His friends could not resist opening the box. They found hundreds of papers inside. Each paper was a note from a student saying that they owed Louis money. By asking his friends to burn the box, Louis released the students from owing him anything. Every "loan" he gave to a poor student was really a free gift.

Many years after he died, Braille's system became the world standard for those with visual impairment. Thanks to his invention, people who are blind can now "see." Braille's system is not only in books. It is embossed on public signs and even on special computer displays that allow blind people to surf the internet. Louis transformed his injury into a passion that empowered people around the world.

Father Angelo Secchi

Astronomer, Pioneer of Astrophysics
(June 28, 1818–February 26, 1878)

Some folks say that science and religion do not go together. Thankfully, Father Angelo Secchi did not think that way. When he was not celebrating Mass or hearing confessions, he operated a telescope and a science lab on top of a church! Angelo showed people that science and religion can go together. He was a priest who used the cutting-edge science of his day to help others.

Angelo was born in Reggio Emilia, Italy. When he was fifteen, he entered the Society of Jesus and studied science and theology. At age twenty-one, he taught math and physics at the Jesuit College in Loreto. In 1847, Angelo was ordained to the priesthood. His first few years in ministry did not go smoothly.

Shortly after his ministry began,

Contemplation of God is one of the noblest occupations of the mind

Catholics in Rome faced a threat. A political revolution gave rise to the Roman Republic, which stood against Catholic leadership. In 1848, an assassin murdered a Catholic leader named Pellegrino Rossi. Father Angelo and other well-known Catholics were pressured to leave the city. Most of the well-known Catholics in Rome feared for their lives. Some priests wore wigs and disguises to secretly continue their ministries. Others fled from Rome, barely escaping with their lives. Even Pope Pius IX was forced to leave Rome for a time.

    The problems in Rome also kept Father Angelo away from the city, but could not stop him from being a priest or a scientist. He went to England and studied and taught at Stonyhurst College. Then he went to the United States and taught at Georgetown University in Washington D.C. While there, Angelo met many scientists. They all shared ideas with each other about stars and teamed up to conduct research.

In 1849, the Roman Republic fell apart, which meant that Catholics could return to Rome. Father Angelo went back to Rome and became the director of an observatory. He had a telescope and a lab installed on the roof of Saint Ignatius Church. Father Angelo became a pioneer in **astrophysics**—the study of stars and objects in space—on top of a Catholic church!

Father Angelo studied magnetism, determined what each planet was made of, and looked at Saturn's rings. He looked at the surface of Mars and took a photo of the moon's craters. Father Angelo photographed the sun during an eclipse and proved that the sun's **corona**—the outermost part of a star's atmosphere—was real and not a trick of the eye. Father Angelo's most lasting discovery had to do with understanding stars through spectroscopy (see **spectroscope**). This involved using a powerful telescope and a prism to **refract**, or break up, light from stars. Once light from a star went through a prism, he could sort the stars by the pattern of the light that he saw. Today, modern scientists still use Father Angelo's main ideas to sort stars by temperature.

Father Angelo applied himself to other problems too. He made sure that water was safe to drink. To keep important buildings from burning down, he put lightning rods on them. He also improved railways and made maps for Rome. Because of his time spent abroad, he made scientific research from the United States known in Italy. He measured air pressure, humidity, temperature, and wind patterns. People around the world gave Father Angelo awards when he set up a telegraphic weather report.

Although Father Angelo was a great scientist, he never ignored his priestly ministry. He defended the Church many times. In 1870, King Victor Emmanuel II took over Rome and forced citizens to swear loyalty to his kingship. Father Angelo refused. He pledged firm loyalty to the pope instead. When officials pressured him, he threatened to leave and to take his work with him. The king's men did not want him to leave, so they softened their stance against priests. Eventually the king met with Catholic leaders and made Rome a friendly place for Catholics again. The pope blessed him, and the king died a good Catholic.

Father Angelo became a member of England's Royal Astronomical Society, the French Academy of Sciences, and Russia's Imperial Academy. In 1870, he wrote a book called *The Sun*. It explained a great deal of useful information about stars and it was translated into many languages. Sadly, some scientists rejected Father Angelo's scientific work because of his Catholic beliefs. Today, scientists rightly recognize him as a pioneer of astrophysics. He is credited for inventing a star classification system and making new discoveries about comets, the sun, and Mars.

Father Angelo wanted to bring science and religion together, so he arranged for all of his scientific awards to be placed at the altars of saints. A crater on the moon, a crater on Mars, and an asteroid have all been named for this great priest and scientist.

Father Léon Provancher

Father of Natural History
(March 10, 1820–March 23, 1892)

I HAVE NEVER ENVISIONED GREEN MEADOWS GOLDEN HARVESTS OR SILENT FORESTS

Great thinkers are not always blessed with a large amount of scientific education or high-tech gear. Does that mean that they cannot make a difference in the world of science? Not at all! For many years, Father Léon Provancher's "laboratory" was only a notepad, a pencil, and the great Canadian outdoors. Still, he became one of the most important natural scientists of North America.

WITHOUT FEELING

Léon was born in the province of Québec, Canada. He grew up in a large family with nine siblings. As a boy, Léon loved being outside. He spent many days climbing trees and looking closely at them, as well as at plants, shells, and stones. He collected bugs and was amazed by their tiny parts. One day, some men were digging a well and Léon noticed a fossil of a shellfish. The fossil left an impression on him and his interest in nature only grew.

In 1834, Léon entered a seminary to prepare for the priesthood. He came across a book in the library about **botany**—the study of plants. Léon could not put the book down. Once he finished reading the book, he identified all of the plants growing around the seminary. He went to nearby parks, meadows, and green spaces to see all the different types of plants. He won the seminary's awards for **horticulture** almost every year while studying to become a priest. He was ordained in 1844 and became a parish priest after his ordination.

For the next thirty years, Father Léon served in many ways. He led pilgrimages to the Holy Land, took care of sick people, and helped churches pay back money they owed. In 1865, Father Léon brought the Third Order of Saint Francis to his parish. This was for lay people who wanted to live the Franciscan spirit. Father Léon and Saint Francis of Assisi were kindred spirits: They both loved nature!

Father Léon continued to explore Canadian wildlife and found many flora (plants) and fauna (animals) that had never been studied before.

In 1868, Father Léon started a monthly magazine called *Le Naturaliste canadien [The Canadian Naturalist]*. The magazine described new plants and bugs that no one had taken the time to notice. It was the first French scientific journal in North America. Father Léon wrote many of the articles and edited the magazine for twenty years. Father Léon did not get much financial help to do his research and faced challenges from those who did not consider him a real scientist. Some people thought that since he had few resources, he could not do quality research. They were wrong!

During his career, Father Léon identified over one thousand new bugs. He wrote three long books that described every known kind of bug in Canada. Father Léon became a world-class expert on **hymenoptera**—a group of insects that includes ants, wasps, and bees. He had the most complete bug collection in North America.

Father Léon's health began to decline in the early 1890s. He went to a town called Cap-Rouge (Cape Red), where he died. Today, Father Léon is honored in Canada for his many achievements. Many streets, a museum, a swamp area, and a building at the University of Québec all bear his name.

THE MORE I STUDY NATURE THE MORE I STAND AMAZED AT THE WORK OF THE CREATOR

Louis Pasteur

Founder of Microbiology
(December 27, 1822–September 28, 1895)

It was a hot summer day in Paris, 1885, when a vicious dog attacked nine-year-old Joseph Meister. The dog bit the boy in fourteen places, leaving him with a deadly disease called **rabies**. When Joseph's mother found out, she panicked. At this time, rabies had no cure. Joseph's mother quickly tracked down a famous scientist named Louis Pasteur to see if he could save her son.

Louis Pasteur was born in a small town called Dole in eastern France. As a child, he enjoyed drawing, painting, and thinking deeply. However, school was a challenge for him. He received low grades and his teachers grew frustrated with him. Louis went to college to study science, but he struggled and dropped out. After some time, he gave college a second try but he failed his final exam and did not graduate.

SCIENCE BRINGS MEN NEARER TO GOD

Few people expected Louis to amount to much. Still, he did not give up. He took a whole year to study and finally earned his science degree in 1842. He did not stop there. In 1845 he earned a master's degree in science, and in 1847, he earned his doctorate. The struggling student who once failed his exam became a great **chemistry** professor!

Louis knew that germs and bacteria caused health problems, so he looked for ways to fight them. He studied microscopic organisms and developed **pasteurization**. This process involved heating liquids and then quickly cooling them to kill germs. It made drinks, such as milk, safer to consume. (The milk we consume today is pasteurized.) Louis founded the branch of science we now call **microbiology**. He became known throughout France for his terrific problem-solving mind.

In 1849, Louis married a woman named Marie. The couple had five children and raised them in the Catholic faith. Because of his hope in God and his scientific background, he was the perfect person to help Joseph, the boy who had been infected with rabies.

Fortunately, Louis was already working on a vaccine for rabies in his lab. He had found a cure that worked on dogs, but had not yet successfully tested it on humans. Louis saw Joseph's mother crying over her sick child and, with her permission, injected the boy with the experimental vaccine. Louis and the mother waited three long weeks to see if the cure would work. To the surprise of other scientists and the extreme joy of his mother, Joseph completely recovered! Joseph was thankful for the rest of his life. He grew up and became a janitor at the Pasteur Institute. He gladly told the story of how Louis saved his life to visitors and guests.

Louis improved medicine in many ways. He insisted that doctors sterilize their instruments before performing surgery. He also helped in developing a vaccine for **anthrax**—a very dangerous disease caused by bacteria. He disproved the false belief of spontaneous generation—the idea that life could begin without something causing it to begin.

As a Catholic man of faith, Louis used his scientific skills to serve others. He felt that when people search for the truth about science and nature, they are really searching for God. He also said that studying science brings people closer to understanding their Creator. He suffered a stroke in 1894, had serious complications, and died the following year.

Father Gregor Mendel

Father of Modern Genetics
(July 20, 1822–January 6, 1884)

Man must contribute his minimum work and God gives the rest

Some people seek fame and fortune after they accomplish something great, but Jesus said, "Blessed are the meek." Few words describe Gregor Mendel better than "meek." As a young man, others did not expect him to become a great scientist. Nevertheless, he made a breakthrough discovery that opened up a whole new branch of science called **genetics**. When he could have become a scientific celebrity, he chose to serve God instead.

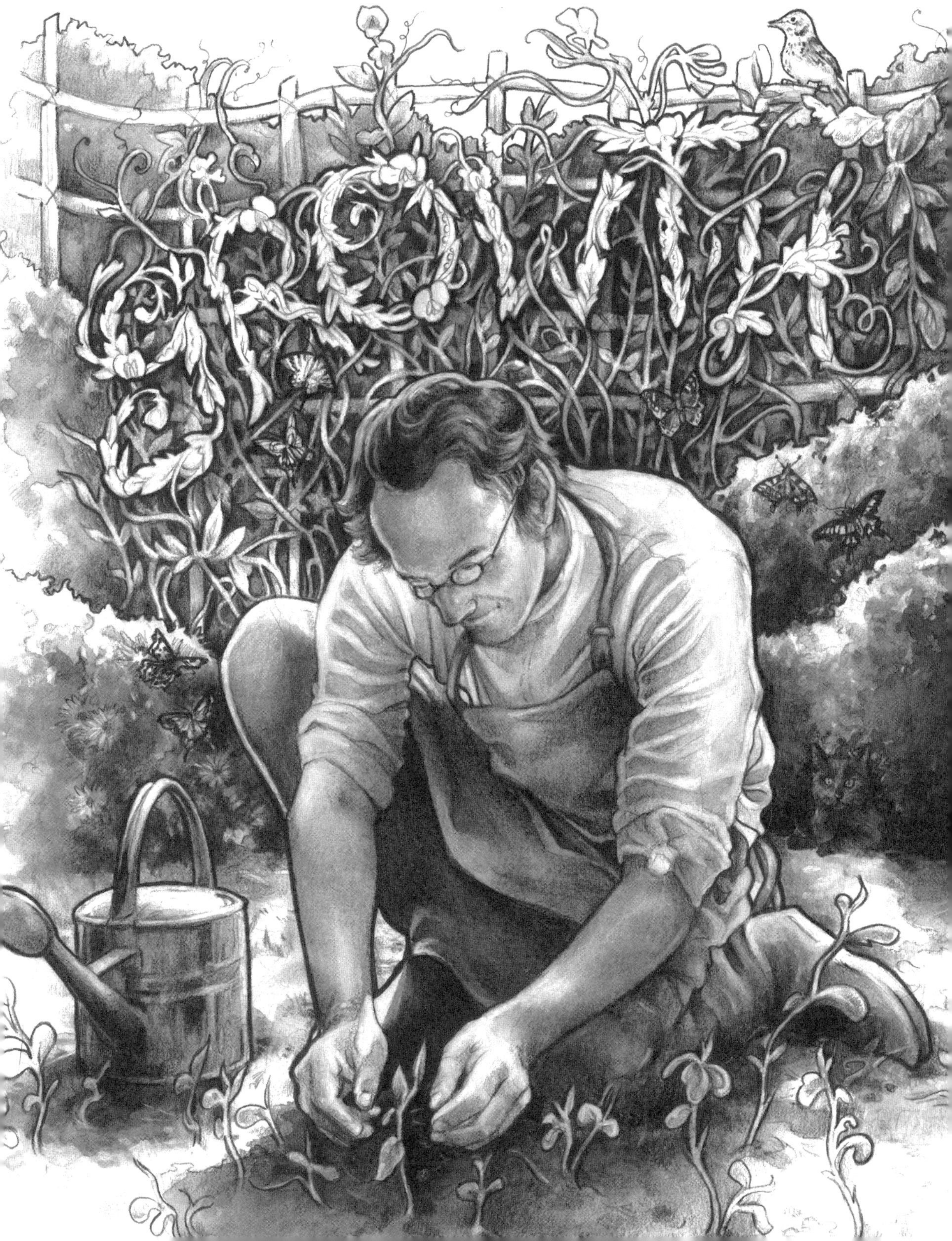

Before he took the name Gregor, Johann Mendel was born in what is now the Czech Republic. As a boy he was interested in gardening, beekeeping, and biology. A Catholic priest recognized Johann's desire to learn and convinced his family to send him to a grammar school. Unfortunately, two obstacles stood in the boy's way. First, his family did not have much money for education. Second, Johann fought depression and illness. His sicknesses often caused him to miss class.

When Johann completed his studies at the grammar school, his father thought that he should return home to work on the farm. But Johann wanted to keep learning. Since he could not afford to attend a university, his sister gave up part of her dowry to cover the costs. While at the university, an illness forced him to miss an entire school year. Even though it took him a long time, he eventually earned a degree in philosophy and physics.

Johann felt called to become a monk. He joined an Augustinian monastery in 1843 and took the name Gregor. His new community saw his talents and gave him space to conduct experiments. He also served as a substitute teacher and later as a science teacher for the local schools. After eight years, they hoped that he could become officially certified as a teacher. They sent him to the University of Vienna in Austria to earn a teaching certificate.

The university made Father Gregor nervous. His professors were not impressed by his work. Father Gregor failed his exams and returned to the monastery without a teaching certificate. Rather than accepting failure, Father Gregor focused on his faith and his work. Little did anyone know that his discoveries would eventually be known by the entire scientific world!

Before Father Gregor's work, scientists knew little about genetics. They understood that ancestors passed traits on to their offspring. For instance, a seed from a red flower was likely to produce a red flower. But they had no way of guessing which traits would be passed on if the ancestors had different traits. No one could explain why a child might have blonde hair while both of her parents have brown hair. Father Mendel was intrigued by this puzzle and he wanted to solve it. He spent nearly ten years working on it. He closely studied the traits of mice, honeybees, and plants. Then, he carefully observed which of those traits were passed on to the offspring. He looked for patterns in the results. He used pea pods to make model systems. Then, he made his greatest discovery.

He carefully analyzed the seed shape, seed color, flower color, and plant height of thousands of pea plants. Father Mendel found consistent results and drew new conclusions about genetics. He used math, logic, and science to successfully identify dominant traits and recessive traits. In 1865, he presented his findings to the Natural History Society. His work helped answer many other questions about genetics.

Father Gregor spent the rest of his days as the **abbot** of his monastery. He was passionate about his Christian faith and sought every opportunity to share it with others. His fellow monks said that he was friendly and assisted anyone who asked for help. Father Gregor's work was not fully understood until some time after his death. Eventually scientists around the world recognized its importance. Today students still use Father Gregor's ideas when they chart **Punnett squares**, which are based on his findings. Father Gregor is now known as the father of modern genetics.

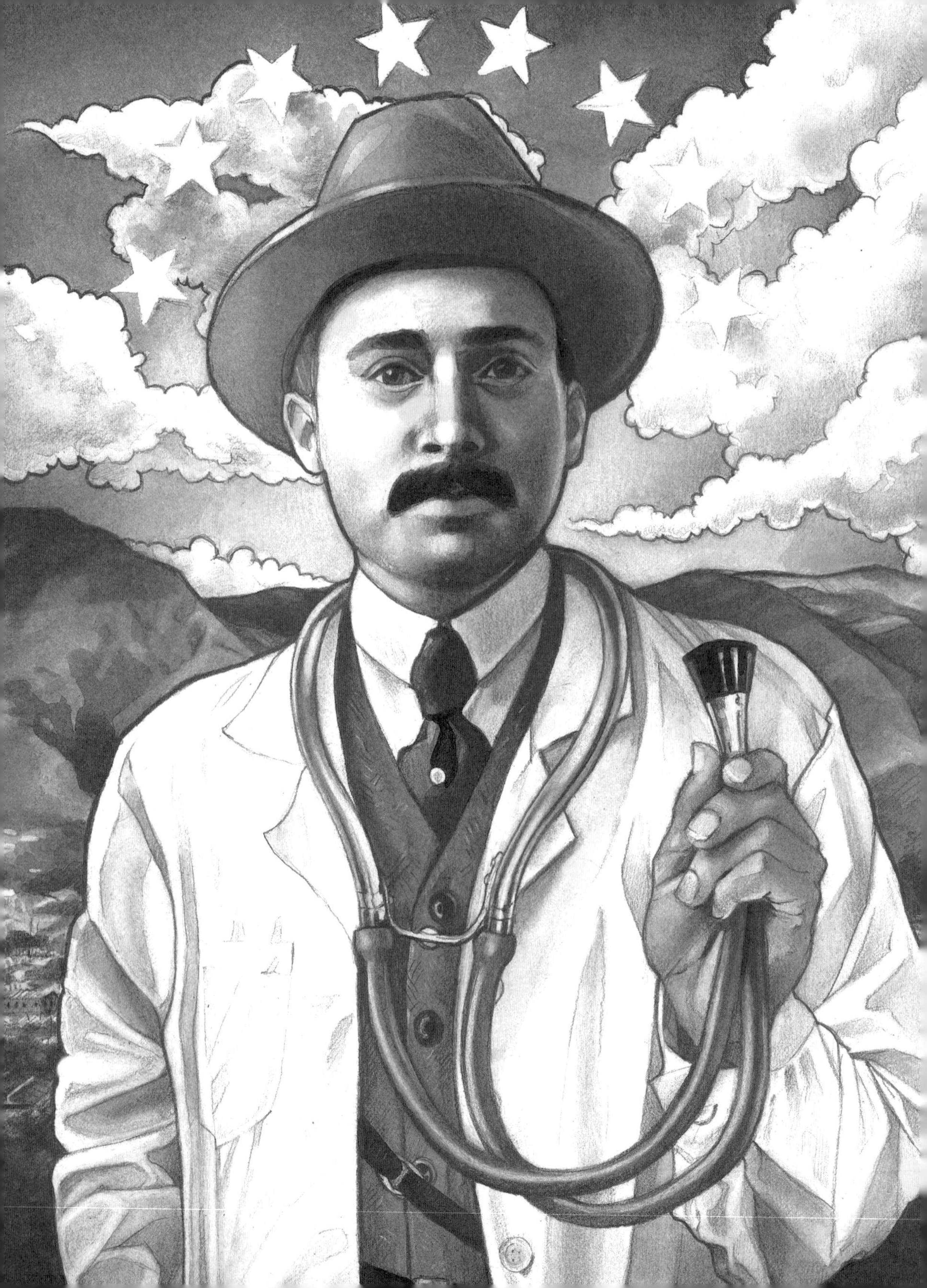

There is an infinitely wise and powerful being... ...creator of the marvelously ordered universe.

Blessed José Gregorio Hernández

Doctor of the Poor
(October 26, 1864–June 29, 1919)

If you walked through the busy streets of La Pastora, in Caracas, Venezuela, you would see pictures of the same person over and over again. A man with a mustache, wearing a suit or a lab coat, is shown on flags, wall paintings, and street signs. This is the beloved local hero, Dr. José Gregorio Hernández.

José was born in Isnotu, a small town in Venezuela, in 1864. His family was Catholic, and he had six younger siblings. His parents owned a shop that sold medical supplies. José's father was not a doctor, but he knew about common illnesses and how to treat them with herbs. José also took interest in medicine. By the time he was thirteen years old, José knew that he wanted to become a doctor.

We call this being God.

José moved to Caracas to attend school there. He won academic awards and even helped teach other students math. He graduated in 1882 with a degree in philosophy. Then he enrolled at the Central University of Venezuela to study medicine.

The next school he attended was the Pasteur Institute in Paris, France. The Pasteur Institute was founded by the Catholic scientist Louis Pasteur. While in Paris, José worked with leading doctors and scientists. He felt that he had a responsibility to bring the latest medical knowledge back to Venezuela. He became a doctor in 1888 and continued his studies in laboratories in Berlin, New York, and Madrid.

In 1890, José heard the news that his father had passed away. He was sad that he was not home in Caracas during his father's last days. He could have lived a comfortable life in Europe with the money he would inherit from his father. Instead, he chose to give all that away. He returned home to share his medical knowledge.

José told the government of Venezuela about the things he had learned from the world's most ground-breaking laboratories. He convinced them to build their own state-of-the-art laboratory in the Caracas hospital. He worked with the government to buy lab equipment and to make sure that the people of Venezuela could get the best medical treatment available. Venezuelan leaders created a new job for José. In 1891, he began work as the leader of the new **pathology**, **physiology**, and **bacteriology** departments at the Central University of Venezuela.

José became well known for bringing modern medicine to Caracas, but didn't let his fame change how he saw people. He spent time with poor and needy people as well as the rich and famous. José followed the example of Jesus by caring for the poor and sick. He often treated patients who had no money, and he even bought medicine for them. This earned him the nickname "Doctor of the Poor."

People sensed that José was a holy man and said that God was working through him.

By 1907, José retired from his university position. He was not married. He decided to enter a religious order in Italy to live for God in a special way. However, the life was too difficult for his health, so José returned to Venezuela.

José helped his community through multiple epidemics over the next ten years. The Spanish Flu particularly affected the people of Venezuela. Although this flu was dangerous and contagious, José continued to treat and pray for patients.

On June 29, 1919, after attending Mass, José was bringing medicine to a sick woman when a car struck and killed him. On the day of his funeral Mass, many thousands of people went out onto the streets, crying, "Our saint is gone!" However, José's story doesn't end with his death. Stories of José helping people continued to be told over the years.

In 2017, a robber shot a ten-year-old girl in the head. Doctors said that the girl would be brain damaged and unable to walk if she survived. Her mother prayed for José to intercede from heaven. The girl completely recovered!

José was declared Blessed in April 2021. Pope Francis described José as a model of service and compared him to the Good Samaritan. Today, José is honored throughout Venezuela and around the world

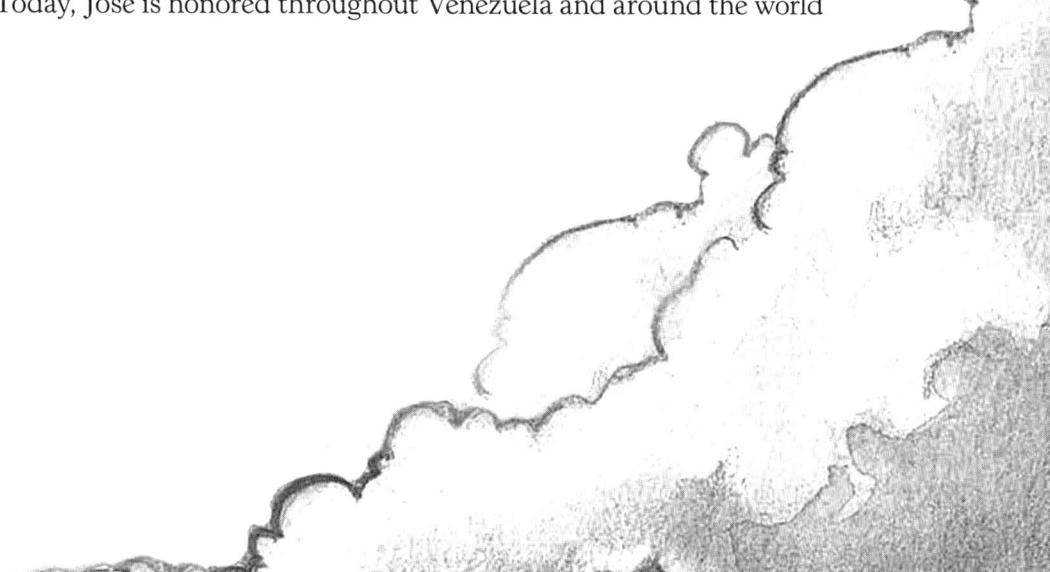

ABOVE ALL, I AM A CATECHIST.

Adrian Atiman

Survivor of Slavery, Missionary Doctor
(c. 1865–April 24, 1956)

In 1876, a group of Catholic priests walked in a slave market in Northern Algeria. These Missionaries of Africa were called "White Fathers" because of the color of their robes. They did what they could to work against slavery by buying some boys in order to free them. They wanted them to have a future of freedom and hope. They didn't know that one of these boys would grow up to be a famous doctor and be awarded medals from several countries. He would also be a **catechist** who would lead many to have faith in Jesus.

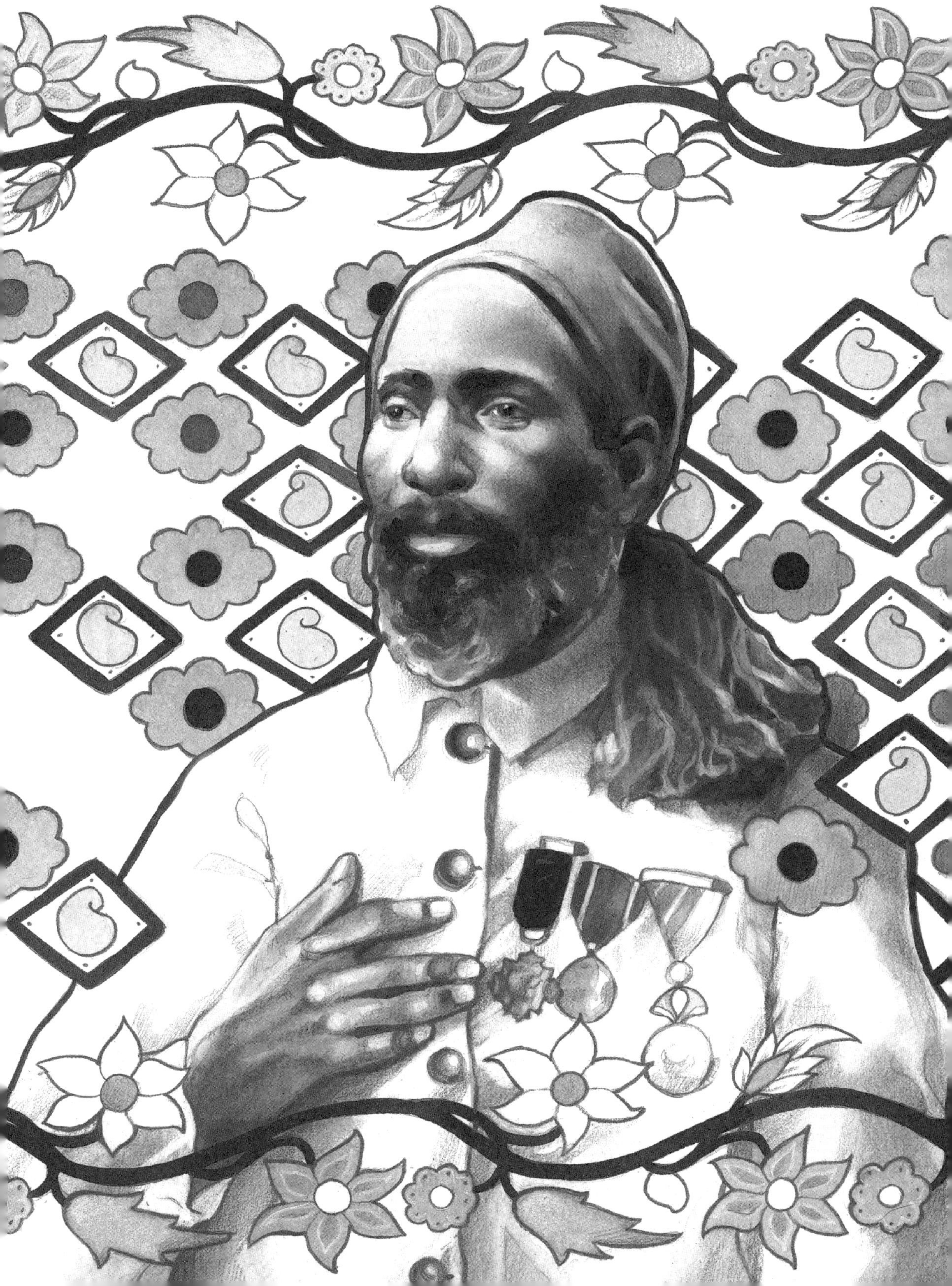

That boy, Adrian Atiman, was born in a village in what is now the country of Mali, West Africa, sometime around 1865. He was kidnapped, taken across the desert, and sold into slavery at age nine or ten. Adrian and the other boys freed by the Missionaries of Africa went to live at an orphanage.

Archbishop Charles Lavigerie was the founder of the Missionaries of Africa. When he met Adrian, he could tell that he was a quick learner and helped him enroll in school. Adrian had a lot of catching up to do! He worked hard at his studies and quickly caught up with his peers. During this time, Adrian became interested in the Christian faith and wanted to be baptized.

In 1881, Adrian went to study medicine at the University of Malta. For this, he had to learn Italian. During his time there, he also studied the Catholic faith and was baptized by Lavigerie. In 1888, around the time Adrian finished his studies, he visited Lavigerie and Pope Leo XIII in Rome.

Lavigerie knew many areas of Africa needed medical doctors and Catholic catechists. When he looked at the incredibly smart Adrian, he saw someone who could be both! Adrian volunteered to go with a group of missionaries to Central Africa.

In 1889, Adrian arrived in Karema, a settlement on the shore of huge Lake Tanganyika, in what is now the country of Tanzania. He earned the trust of the community by caring for people who had escaped slavery and were in very poor health.

Whenever he was practicing medicine, Adrian made it a point to talk about God. He helped his patients be healed in body and in spirit. He wanted to be a catechist first and a doctor second. When he was successful, he gave the credit to God. He went to Mass every morning. People remembered that he stayed to pray while everyone else left for breakfast.

Soon, people were traveling for days to be treated by this missionary doctor. He took care of a wide variety of illnesses, including smallpox and sleeping sickness, as well as wounds from spears, lions, and crocodiles. He had not trained as a surgeon, but he taught himself what he needed to know, keeping up with advances in medicine by reading medical journals. It is said that Adrian was the only doctor in an area the size of the state of Texas.

Adrian's knowledge of medicine was in high demand. He was offered high-paying medical jobs, but he always refused. He trusted that God would protect and provide for him, just as he had when Adrian was a child.

Over time, Adrian became a legend across all of Africa, but he remained humble. He received awards and honors from the French, Belgian, and British governments. Three popes—Pope Leo XIII, Pope Pius XI, and Pope Pius XII—honored him for his service to the Catholic Church.

Adrian was about ninety years old when he died at the mission at Karema in 1956. Though people around the world knew of his heroic medical service, Adrian often said, "Above all, I am a catechist."

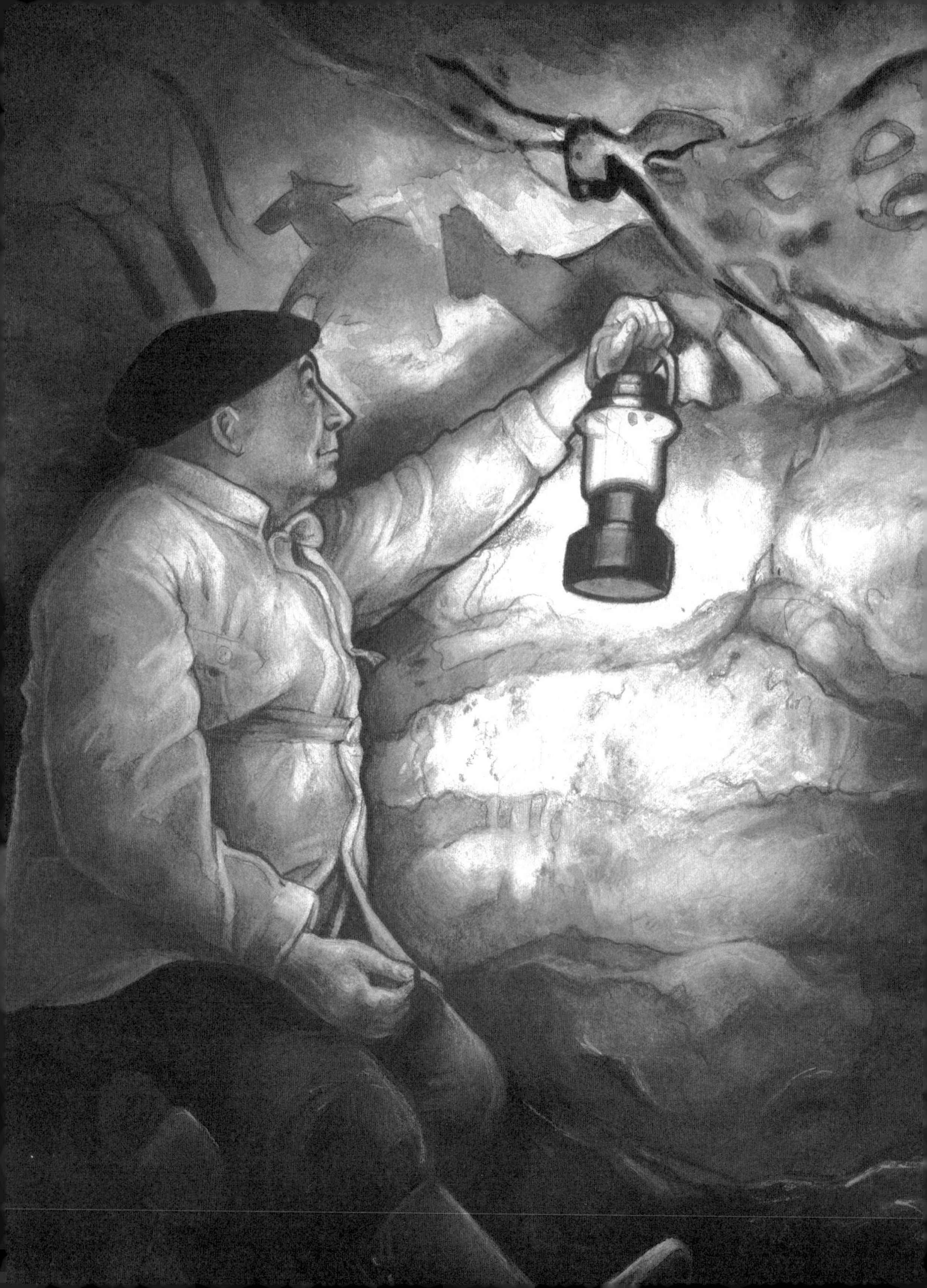

Father Henri Breuil

Archaeologist and Natural Scientist

(February 28, 1877–August 14, 1961)

Humans did not write words until sometime around 3400 BC. Still, historians know many things about the lives of prehistoric man. (Prehistory is the time before humans could write things down.) Experts can tell you where early humans traveled, which animals they hunted, and some of the things they believed. But how do historians know what life was like before people could write about it? The answer involves old artwork and a French priest named Father Henri Breuil.

Henri was born in Normandy, France. He loved to draw when he was a boy. As he grew, he carried a sketchbook everywhere he went and could accurately sketch anything he saw. After graduating from the College of Saint Vincent, he become a priest. He entered the seminary in 1895 and was ordained in 1897.

One summer, Father Henri took a tour of an ancient city in southwest France surrounded by cliffs. While exploring, he met an **archeologist** named Edouard Piette. Henri learned that early humans painted pictures on cave walls and carved shapes into stones. These pictures held lots of information, but it was hard to understand what they meant. Father Henri was amazed and wanted to learn more. For the next several years, Piette taught Father Henri archaeology. Piette also paid him to draw objects that they found on their journeys.

In 1898, Father Henri explored a rock shelter where early human skeletons were found. The next year, he looked over collections of artifacts in England. In 1900, Father Henri was in a difficult position. He was a new priest who wanted to serve the Church. But his scientific career was taking off. Could he be both a successful archeologist and a priest?

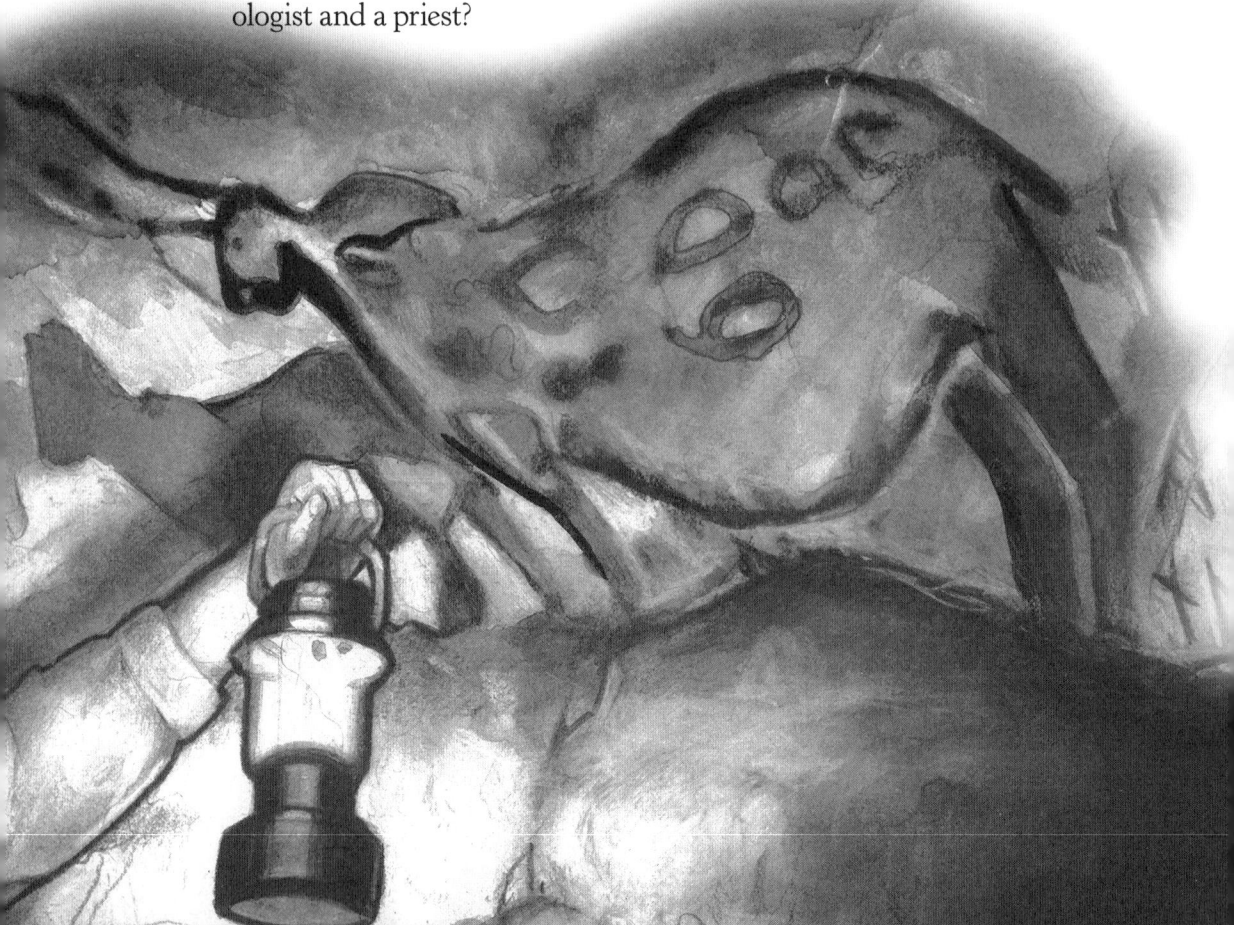

Henri's bishop thought that his scientific work was important. He allowed Henri to keep studying and did not assign him to a parish. Still, Henri was expected to live out his priestly ministry. He took his Catholic faith with him in the scientific field.

Henri learned all he could about the **Stone Age** and the **Bronze Age**. In 1903, he earned a degree in natural science from the University of Paris. Henri found patterns and clues in cave art that revealed information about early man's way of life. Sometimes his colleagues were puzzled that such a respected scientist was also a man of faith. Henri told them that science was no challenge to faith. He said that a correct understanding of the Bible does not contradict new scientific discoveries. Over time, Henri earned the respect of some non-Catholic scientists.

In 1940, four teenagers followed a wandering dog into a cave in southern France. They discovered that the walls of the cave were covered with more than six hundred works of prehistoric art. The cave drawings had not been seen in seventeen thousand years. Henri was the first archaeologist on the site. He carefully studied and copied the art. His drawings and writings were published around the world. This led to a greater understanding of early humans.

Henri shared a system that helped people organize and understand many objects from the Ice Age. He became a professor at the College of France where he taught for eighteen years. When he died in 1961, he belonged to nineteen scientific groups. The U.S. National Academy of Sciences gave him a medal for his work with cave drawings. Henri was a man of faith and science whose work helped us understand human history.

Saint Giuseppe Moscati

Medical Doctor and Chemist
(July 25, 1880–April 12, 1927)

Saint Giuseppe Moscati used medical science as a religious calling. He cared for people's bodies as well as their souls.

Giuseppe was born in Italy, the seventh of nine children in a deeply Catholic home. When he was twelve, his older brother suffered a head injury that caused him to stay home. Sadly, the brother never fully recovered. Giuseppe often helped to take care of him and was inspired to learn more about treating the sick.

A few years later, Giuseppe studied surgery at the University of Naples. While there, he went to Mass daily. He graduated with honors and earned a degree in medicine. He became a doctor and director at a hospital near Mount Vesuvius.

Mount Vesuvius was once a very active volcano, but it had not been considered dangerous for many years. People thought that it was safe to live nearby. In early April 1906, Mount Vesuvius had a sudden, major eruption. It spewed lava and ruined buildings and claimed lives. Ash piled up all around. Giuseppe knew that his hospital patients were in danger. Instead of fleeing, Giuseppe led efforts to transport people to safety. He made sure that all patients,

BLESSED IF WE ARE WE
REMEMBER

THAT WE HAVE NOT ONLY
BODIES TO CURE
BUT ALSO
ETERNAL SOULS

especially the elderly and disabled, were carried to a safe location. Moments after the last patient escaped, the weight of the ash caused the hospital roof to fall in. People called Giuseppe a hero, but he directed credit to the others who helped as well.

Over the next few years, Giuseppe's status as a scientist grew. He continued to study medicine and other doctors often asked for his advice. In 1911, Giuseppe became a member of the Royal Academy of Surgical Medicine. That year he also earned a doctorate while studying the chemistry of the human body.

The University of Naples named Giuseppe a professor. He taught about harmful chemicals and the causes of sickness. He also made discoveries about **insulin** (a hormone that controls the amount of sugar in blood). His work continues to help people today.

Giuseppe was kind. He treated poor patients for free. He said that God wanted him to share his gifts. He noticed that many of his poor patients suffered from **cholera**—a sickness caused by a certain bacteria often found in unclean water. Giuseppe shared ideas with city officials about keeping water clean. It helped improve the lives of many people, but especially the poor. Giuseppe treated thousands of injured Italian soldiers during World War I. He also encouraged his patients to receive the sacraments and prayed with them.

On April 12, 1927, Giuseppe went about his tasks as usual. He took care of patients in the hospital. Feeling tired, he sat down in a chair and quietly died. News of his death touched many people who admired him. A newspaper wrote that Giuseppe was a great teacher, a true follower of Christ, and proof that religion and science can go together.

After his death, many people claimed to experience miracles of healing performed by Giuseppe. The miracle for his **canonization** was the cure of Giuseppe Fusco, a young man dying of leukemia. His mother had a dream that a man in a white coat came and treated her son. Afterward, the boy was completely healed. Later on, her parish priest showed the mother a photo of Giuseppe and she recognized him as the man from her dream.

On October 25, 1987, Pope Saint John Paul II named Giuseppe a saint. He is a patron saint of doctors. His feast day is November 16.

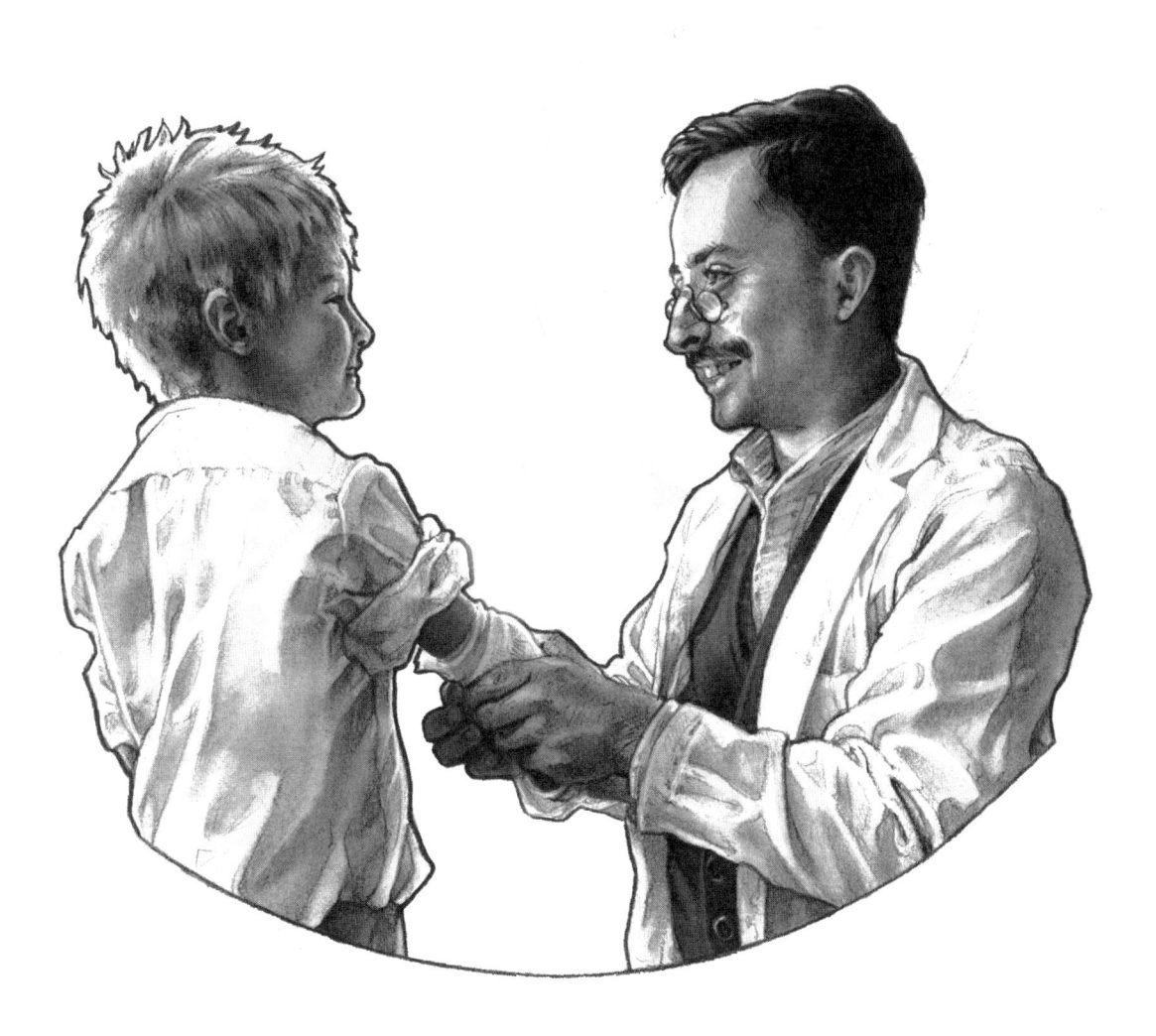

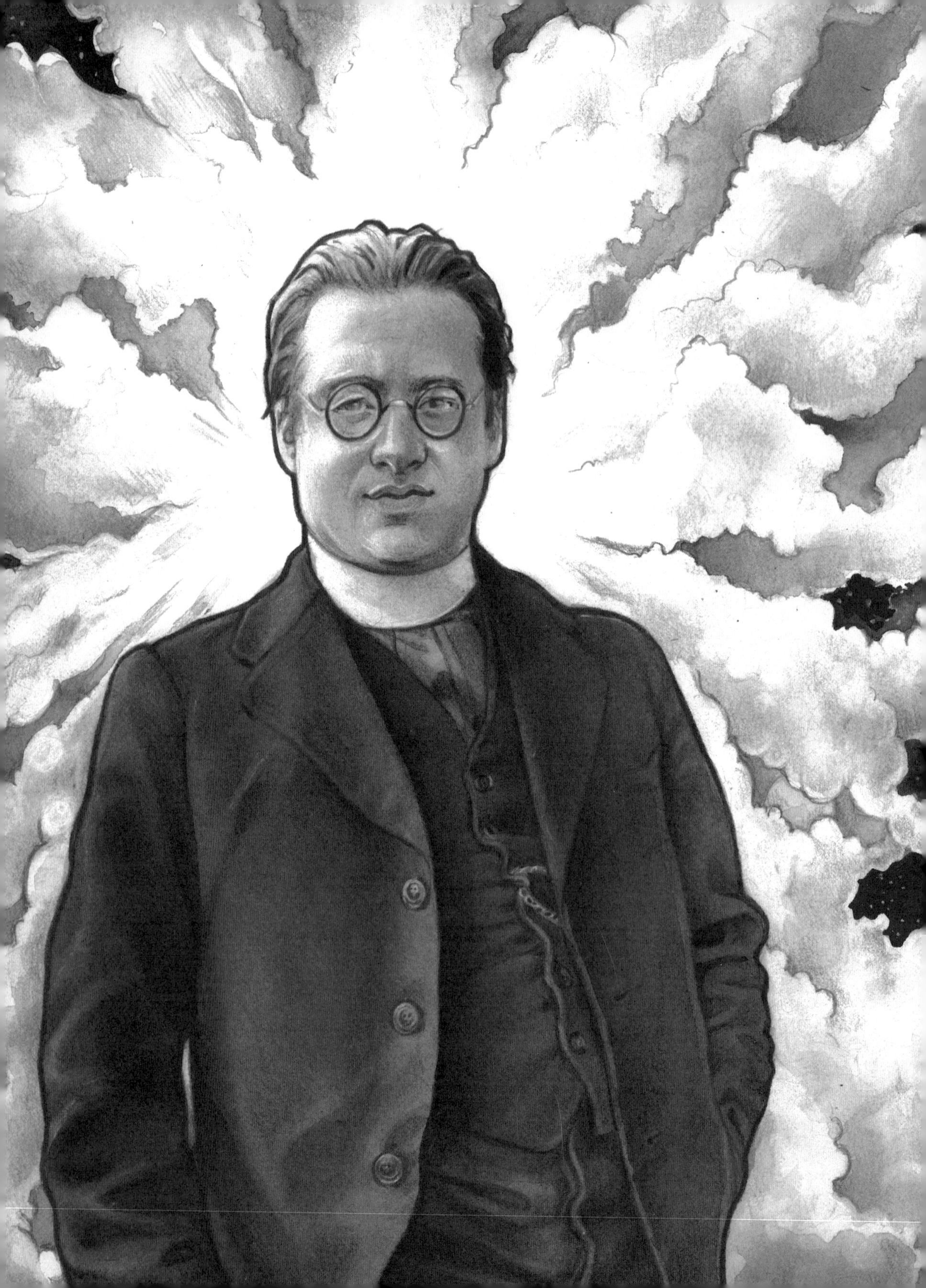

There is no conflict between religion and science

Father Georges Lemaître

Father of the Big Bang Theory
(July 17, 1894–June 20, 1966)

For a long time, scientists thought that the universe was fixed in its size. Some thought that it did not have a beginning. They believed that it always existed and was merely matter with no origin from God. This idea clashed with the Catholic belief that God created the universe. It seemed as though faith and science could not agree. Today, however, scientists know that the universe had a beginning and is still getting bigger. It has been growing ever since it began! Scientists now know all of this because a Catholic priest, Father Georges Lemaître, came up with an idea about the start of the universe that was provable with science and lined up with the Catholic faith.

Born in Belgium, Georges was a boy who loved figuring out how things worked. He had a talent for science and math as well as a love of his faith. Sometimes people told him that faith and science could not get along, but he disagreed.

After finishing school, Georges served in the Army during World War I. After the war, he studied mathematics and received a doctorate in 1920. He also decided to become a priest and was ordained in 1923.

Georges earned advanced degrees in math, science, and physics from the finest schools in the world. He studied at the University of Cambridge in the United Kingdom, and at Harvard University and the Massachusetts Institute of Technology (MIT) in Cambridge, Massachusetts. While serving as a priest, Father Georges became a professor at the Catholic University of Leuven in Flanders, Belgium.

Father Georges heard theories that the universe was growing. His theory, which later became known as the Big Bang theory, took the idea even further. He said that if the universe was expanding, then it must have once been squished in a much smaller form. He said that the universe was once packed into what he called a "cosmic egg." According to his theory, this egg suddenly burst open with a giant bang and the universe quickly spread out. This giant explosion continues to give the universe its growing shape today. In 1927, he shared his ideas and people took notice.

The Big Bang theory was a big deal for both scientific and religious groups. It provided common ground where a lot of people thought there was none. For scientists, it explained that our universe was growing and why. For the religious, it supported the idea that our universe had a beginning and did not always exist. Pope Pius XII said that the theory supported the belief that God created the universe.

At first, a famous scientist named Albert Einstein did not agree with the Big Bang theory. But over time, his views changed and he came to see the merit of some of Father Georges' ideas. Einstein and Father Georges respected one another as scientists. When Father Georges took the stage at a gathering of the world's greatest scientists, he used science and math to explain his ideas. Later on other scientists expanded on the Big Bang theory. Since then, mathematicians have been able to measure the speed of our universe's growth. This measurement tells us that the universe is likely more than 13 billion years old.

Father Georges was honored with many awards. Pope Pius XII, King Leopold III, and scientific groups around the world celebrated the priest's work. In 1936, Father Georges became a member of the pope's team of scientists and later was asked to be its leader. He served in this way for sixteen years. Although he did not win it, Father Georges was nominated for the Nobel Prize in 1954 and again in 1956. After a celebrated career in science and many years of ministry, Father Georges died from cancer. He is remembered as a humble man who viewed both science and religion as honest ways of seeking the truth.

For a long time, the scientific community had forgotten about Father Georges' contribution to the idea that the universe is expanding. The law that describes the provable expansion of our universe was simply known as the Hubble Law, named after the astronomer Edwin Hubble who discovered the law not long after Father Georges. In 2018, however, scientists voted to honor Father Georges by renaming it the **Hubble-Lemaître Law**. A crater on the moon and a small planet are both named after him.

I'M INTERESTED IN DOING ALL I CAN TO ADVANCE KNOWLEDGE

Sister Hilary Ross

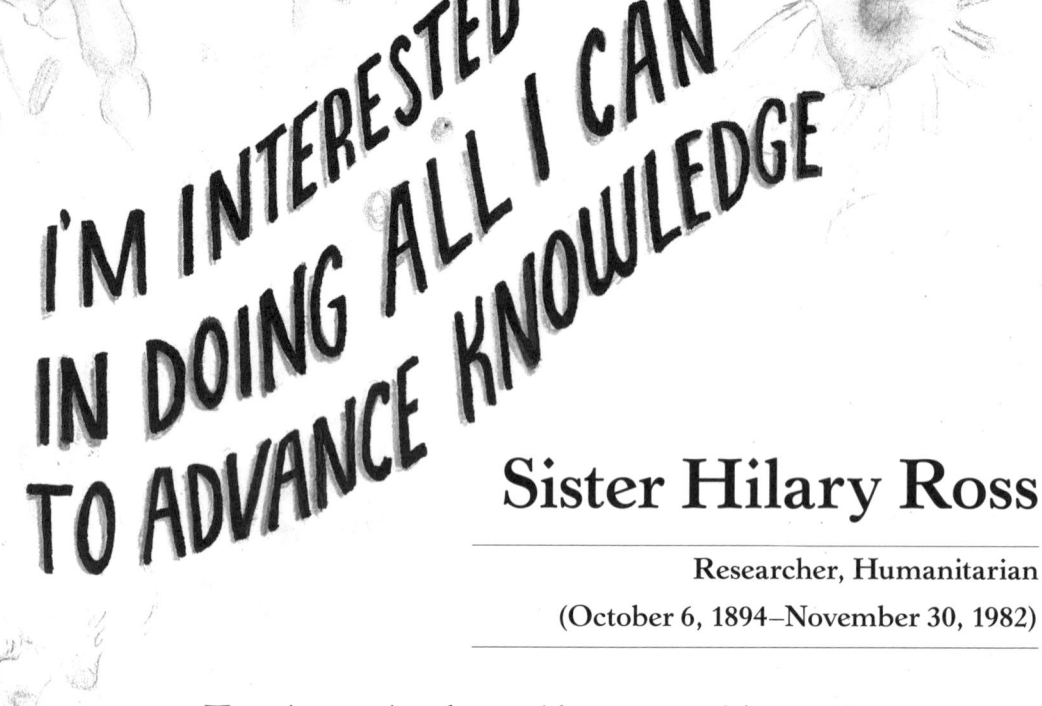

Researcher, Humanitarian
(October 6, 1894–November 30, 1982)

Imagine coming down with a strange sickness. You are cast out from your town. You must change your last name to protect your family.

For too long, this was reality for people who had Hansen's Disease (once called leprosy). Hansen's Disease is an infection caused by bacteria—called *mycobacterium leprae*. The sickness affects a person's skin, nose, eyes, and nerves. It causes large bumps on the skin that can make a person unrecognizable. It can affect fingers and other parts of the body, leaving a person feeling numb and making common tasks nearly impossible to perform. Left untreated, the condition causes people to be disfigured and disabled. Hansen's Disease had no cure until 1941 when a team of medical professionals, including Sister Hilary Ross, finally found it.

Before she became a nun, Mary Ross was born in California. She was the second oldest of her seven siblings in a Protestant home. Her father died in a boating accident in 1905. Shortly after his death, an earthquake destroyed her family's home and belongings. As a teenager, Mary got a job to support her family.

OF THE

Mary worked in a clothing store. One of her co-workers was Catholic and invited Mary to Mass. Mary eventually became Catholic. A little while later, she was called to join a religious order. Mary joined the Daughters of Charity and took the name Sister Hilary.

Shortly after she became a sister, Sister Hilary's community encouraged her to learn medicine. She studied pharmacy at the University of Wisconsin. Around this time, Sister Hilary learned of a need for caretakers to work in a leprosarium in Carville, Louisiana. A leprosarium is a place where people living with Hansen's Disease were kept away from others. Sister Hilary wanted to serve the patients in Carville.

Sister Hilary and her fellow Daughters of Charity wanted to show the patients compassion. They took care of the medical needs of patients and also cared for them as friends. Sister Hilary and the other Daughters of Charity made crafts for the patients, taught them classes, and threw wonderful Christmas parties.

Sister Hilary gave them the best medicine she could, oil from evergreen trees. The oil seemed to help ease some symptoms, but it wasn't a cure. The wrong dosage could also make patients feel sick. Sister Hilary wanted to find something better for her patients.

Sister Hilary met with a doctor who taught her advanced lab methods. She went to Louisiana State University in 1937 and studied Hansen's Disease on a chemical level. She noticed that patients' blood chemistry changed once the disease had become so severe that it affected their fingers and toes. She wrote about these findings and also noticed other changes in the body. With time, doctors made new drugs available and researchers looked for ones that would cure Hansen's Disease.

In 1941, Dr. Guy Faget and Dr. Frank McCreary thought that new sulfone drugs could be used to fight Hansen's Disease. They came to Carville and worked with Sister Hilary. The doctors used her years of research and notes to make decisions about the dosage and treatments. Once they were sure that the drugs were safe, the doctors gave them to the patients. Sister Hilary cared for the patients and watched them closely to keep records of the results of the treatments. Within just six months of receiving the drugs, Sister Hilary saw that her patients were healing. Hansen's Disease had met its match. They had found a cure!

Although there was now a cure, the general public could not believe it. They wanted proof. Sister Hilary took pictures of patients before and after their treatment. Sister Hilary shared these photos with doctors around the world who gathered at a conference to discuss treatment for Hansen's Disease. The images demonstrated that sulfone drugs reversed most of the effects of the disease.

Sister Hilary spent thirty-seven years in Carville helping patients. She became a globally recognized expert on Hansen's Disease. When she was not taking care of patients, she worked to educate the general public about the sickness. In ancient times, the term leprosy was used to describe lots of different skin conditions, and some of these were contagious and even deadly. This led to misunderstandings and myths about Hansen's Disease. Today scientists do not use the word "leper" because of the pain and fear that it still carries. Hansen's Disease does still exist in some parts of the world. However, it is easily curable in countries that have developed health care.

President Eisenhower and many Catholic organizations admired Sister Hilary and her sisters' work. She was given awards from universities and the U.S. Surgeon General. When she was in her late sixties, she moved to Japan. She spent her remaining days taking care of disabled children as a Daughter of Charity.

Takashi Nagai

Pioneer of Radiology, Survivor of the Atomic Bomb, Servant of God
(February 3, 1908–May 1, 1951)

    Takashi Nagai was born in Matsue, Japan, in 1908. As a boy, he dreamed of wearing a **stethoscope** and becoming a medical doctor like his father.

    When Takashi was in high school, he decided that religion was old-fashioned. He rejected his family's **Shinto** faith and became an **atheist**.

    While studying medicine at the Nagasaki Medical University, Takashi admired the work of scientist Blaise Pascal (1623–1662). When he learned that Pascal was Catholic, he was shocked! How could Pascal believe in Catholicism without it contradicting his science? He decided to rent a room from the

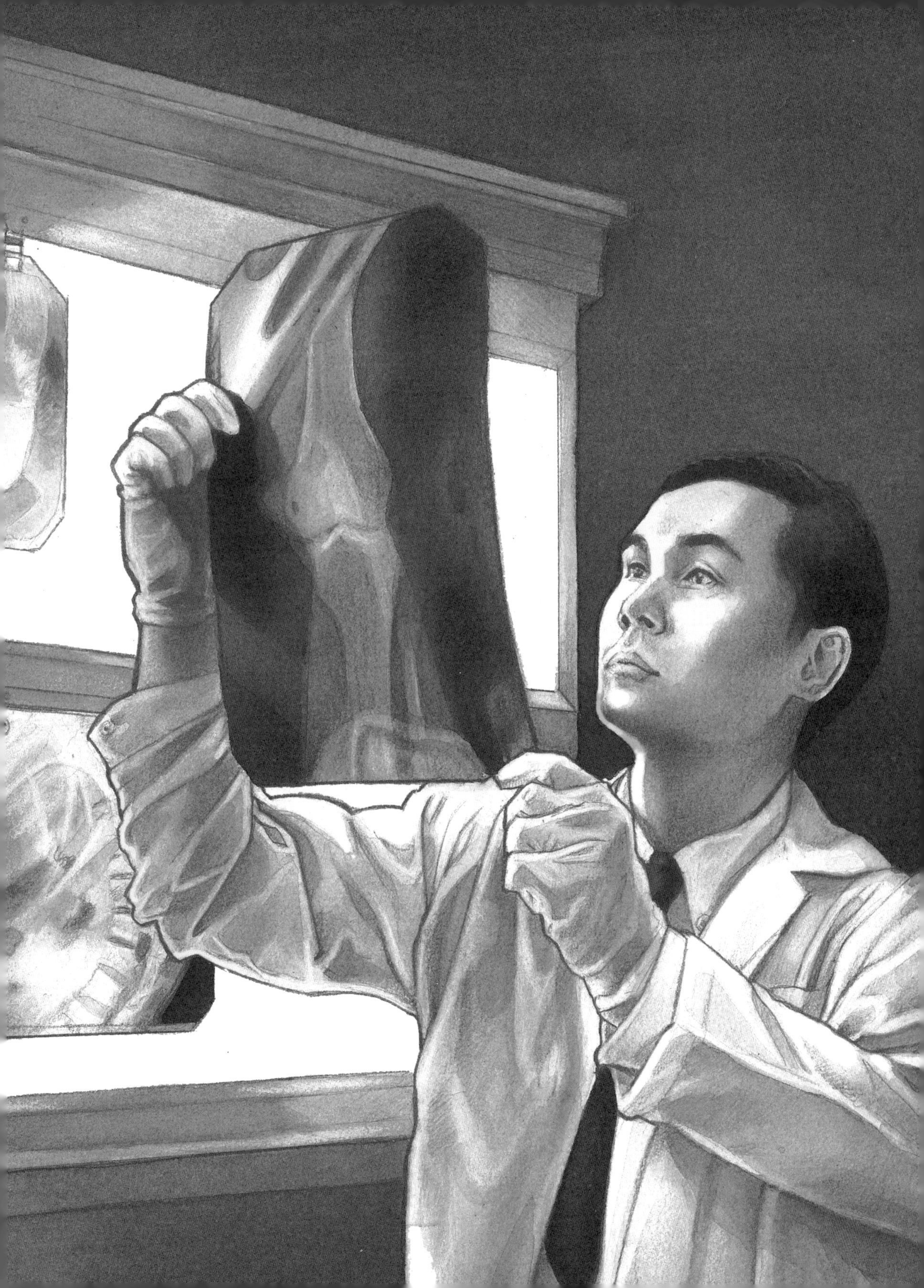

Moriyamas, a Catholic couple. They welcomed Takashi into their home and introduced him to their beautiful daughter, a schoolteacher named Midori.

Takashi finished his studies with top honors. He was chosen to give the University's graduation speech in 1932. However, Takashi spent the night before partying and was too sick to give his speech. He had severe **meningitis** and a buildup of fluid behind his right ear. His hearing was forever damaged.

Takashi was very sad. He knew that he could never use a stethoscope and be a doctor. Then, Takashi was asked to develop the university's radiology department. **X-rays** could be used to quickly find medical problems. However, the radiation from the X-ray machine could make a person very sick. Technicians had not figured out how to protect themselves from X-rays. Even though it was dangerous, Takashi took the job. He learned about atoms, radiology, and nuclear energy.

In 1933, Takashi received orders to join the Japanese military. Midori prayed for his safety. She mailed him gifts, including a book about the Catholic faith, which inspired him. When he returned in 1934, he was baptized and married Midori. They had two children.

Takashi soon became an expert in radiology. He used X-rays to diagnose many patients, including Saint Maximilian Kolbe (1894–1941)! He found a faster way to diagnose **tuberculosis**. His findings were published in medical journals and textbooks. He became the chief of medical staff at the university hospital. Takashi joined the **Saint Vincent de Paul Society** and convinced other doctors to join him on mission trips to care for the sick.

When World War II began, Takashi was called back to the military. He did not like war. He served as a chief surgeon to help people stay alive. In 1941, Japan bombed Pearl Harbor, Hawaii. Many Americans died in the attack. Takashi prayed that war with Americans could be avoided. The Japanese government asked Takashi to help prepare citizens for an attack. Takashi taught people how to take shelter and apply first aid. He also helped build an underground medical center.

In early August of 1945, a powerful bomb hit Hiroshima, Japan. Takashi and Midori feared that Nagasaki might be next. On August 9, their fears came true.

Takashi was working in the underground medical center when an American airplane dropped an atomic bomb on the city. Even underground, Takashi was seriously injured. Thousands of people died. The radiology lab and hospital were destroyed. Schools were gone. The Nagasaki Cathedral was reduced to rubble. Takashi knew his leadership and medical skills were needed.

The radiation from the bomb was still deadly, but Takashi tended to survivors. He exhausted himself by bandaging patients and giving them water. His children survived, but his beloved Midori died while holding a rosary. The destruction caused Japan to surrender and end the war.

Although Takashi was weak, he still helped people. He spoke about hope at a Mass that took place at the site of the destroyed cathedral. After this, he spent more time with his children. He wrote a book describing how the atomic bomb medically affected people. It was the first scientific report of its kind. He also wrote about his experiences and using atomic energy to help and not harm others.

Takashi led the community to rebuild. He encouraged people to construct a new church. Then he helped build a hospital, a school, and an orphanage. In 1946, Takashi had a second chance to give a graduation speech. He reminded his listeners that everyone must work for peace.

He used his money to plant one thousand cherry blossom trees in areas that had been devastated by the bomb. He gave the rest to the hospital and chose to live poorly himself. In his final months, he was surrounded by his children and people from around the world who wanted to meet him. He was visited by the Japanese emperor and many famous people. Pope Pius XII sent Takashi a rosary, which he held as he died on May 1, 1951.

Today, Takashi Nagai is a national Japanese hero. Two museums and a major peace prize are named after him. He is a "Servant of God," the first step toward being canonized a saint.

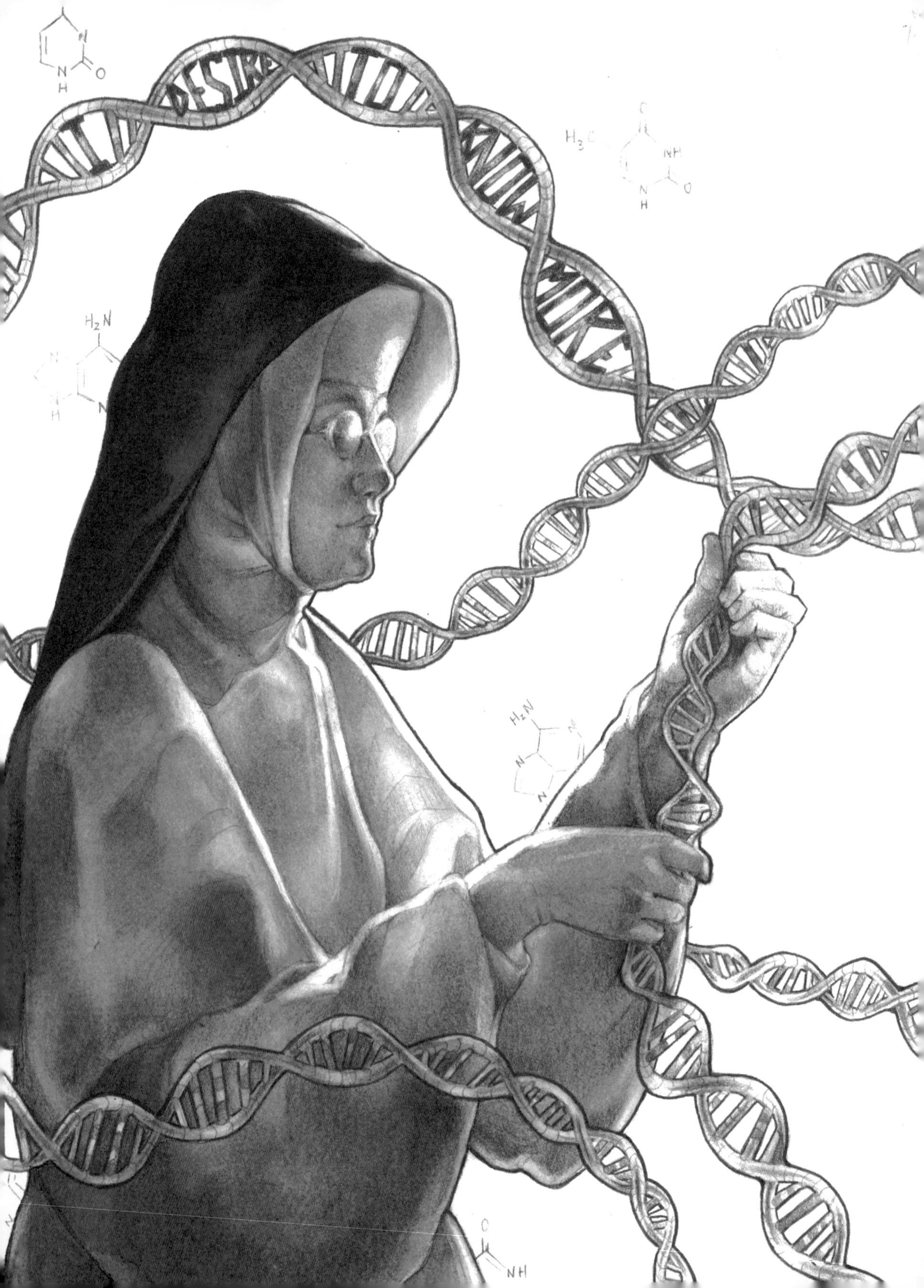

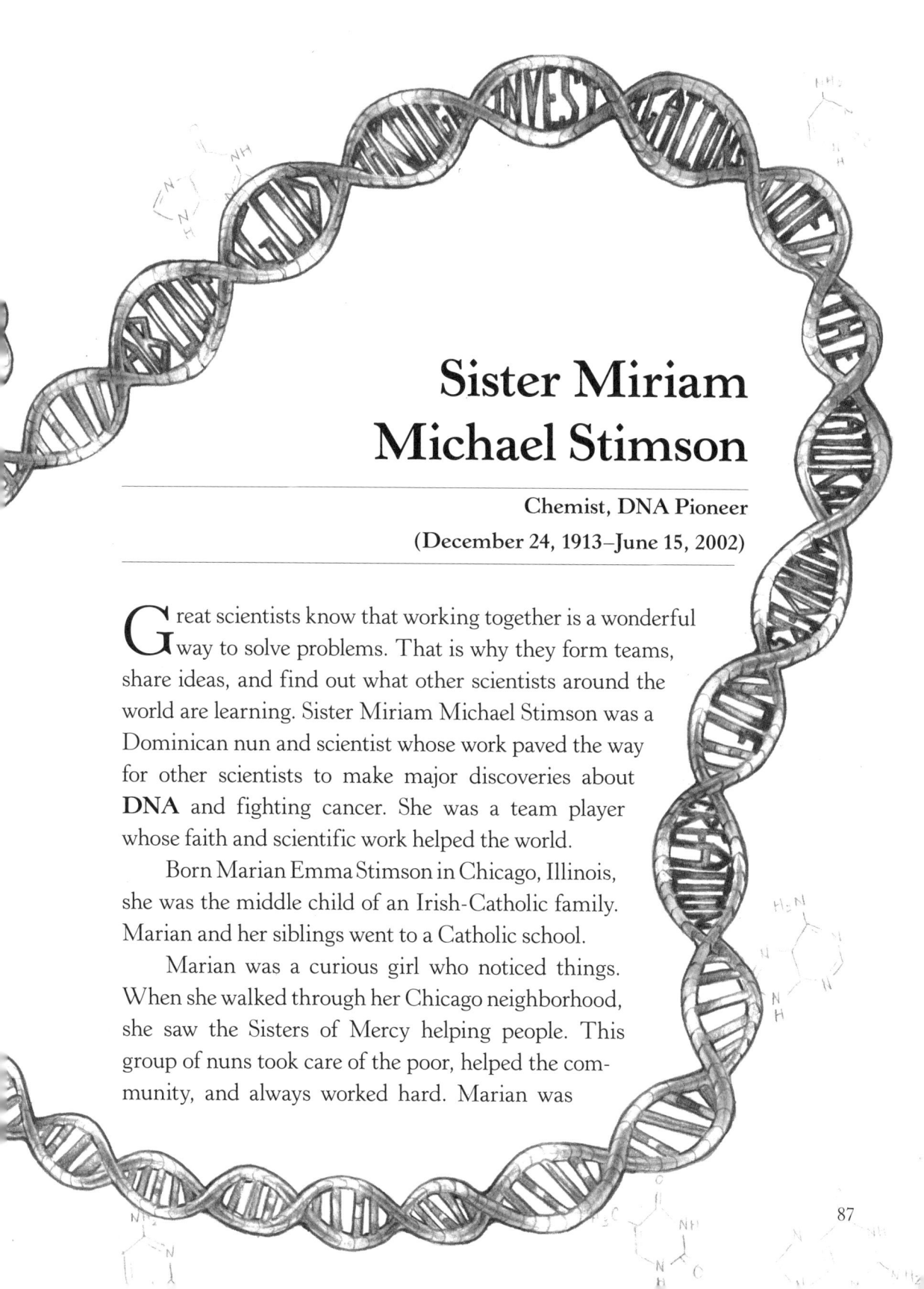

Sister Miriam Michael Stimson

Chemist, DNA Pioneer
(December 24, 1913–June 15, 2002)

Great scientists know that working together is a wonderful way to solve problems. That is why they form teams, share ideas, and find out what other scientists around the world are learning. Sister Miriam Michael Stimson was a Dominican nun and scientist whose work paved the way for other scientists to make major discoveries about **DNA** and fighting cancer. She was a team player whose faith and scientific work helped the world.

Born Marian Emma Stimson in Chicago, Illinois, she was the middle child of an Irish-Catholic family. Marian and her siblings went to a Catholic school.

Marian was a curious girl who noticed things. When she walked through her Chicago neighborhood, she saw the Sisters of Mercy helping people. This group of nuns took care of the poor, helped the community, and always worked hard. Marian was inspired by them and also wanted to help others. She tried her best at school and excelled in science.

Marian's hard work was not limited to school. She had more jobs at home than most kids her age. She took care of sick family members. Her older brother had polio, and her sister Alice had heart problems that left her weak. Marian's mother placed her in charge of caring for the family's newborn twins.

When Marian turned fourteen, her parents sent her and her sister Alice to Saint Joseph Academy, a boarding school in Michigan. After some time at the school, Alice's heart weakened and she died. Marian was very upset over losing her sister. She was about to finish high school and did not know what to do with her life. She sought the guidance of the Dominican sisters who ran the school. They suggested that she continue her studies at Saint Joseph College, today known as Siena Heights University, in Adrian, Michigan. The sisters even helped her pay for her first year.

During her freshman year, Marian grew to love the Dominican way of life. She studied hard and went to Mass daily. She fit right in with the sisters, who keenly studied Scripture, theology, and science. Marian slowly felt called to join the order.

In 1935 Marian entered the Dominicans and changed her name to Sister Miriam Michael. They sent her to earn her master's of Science degree from the Institute of Saint Thomas in Cincinnati, Ohio. She could not have been more pleased!

After earning her master's degree, Sister Miriam became a chemistry professor and researched new information about chemicals and their effects on cells. She used a **spectroscope**—a tool that measures different types of light—to see the molecules that make up cells. She became an expert at using the spectroscope and wanted to teach other scientists how to use it. She wrote a manual and taught lessons.

Sister Miriam knew that fighting diseases like cancer required looking at cells more closely, on a molecular level. In 1939, she opened a lab at Saint Joseph College where scientists could learn about cancer and work toward a cure. Sister Miriam led teams to conduct experiments. She recorded data about **ultraviolet light**—light that is not visible to the human eye. She also explained the effects that certain chemicals have on yeast. Sister Miriam contributed to research that enabled scientists to discover what DNA is made up of. Her research led to new and deeper understanding about the causes of cell damage. It also helped scientists to understand the process of cell division. People around the world noticed her work.

The Sorbonne Institute in Paris invited Sister Miriam to give a lecture. She was the second woman in history to be given this honor. The first was Marie Curie, a physicist who pioneered research in radioactivity. Sister Miriam was a famous scientist, but remained humble. If her students found out about her fame, it was usually after they read about it in a book or magazine.

Sister Miriam also played a major role in developing what is known as the **KBr disk method**—a method of preparing cell samples to be looked at under a microscope. This work made it possible for other scientists such as Rosalind Franklin, James Watson, Francis Crick, and Maurice Wilkins to discover the double-helix shape of DNA. This understanding has changed the way that scientists fight cancer today. Sister Miriam also helped develop treatments for healing wounds.

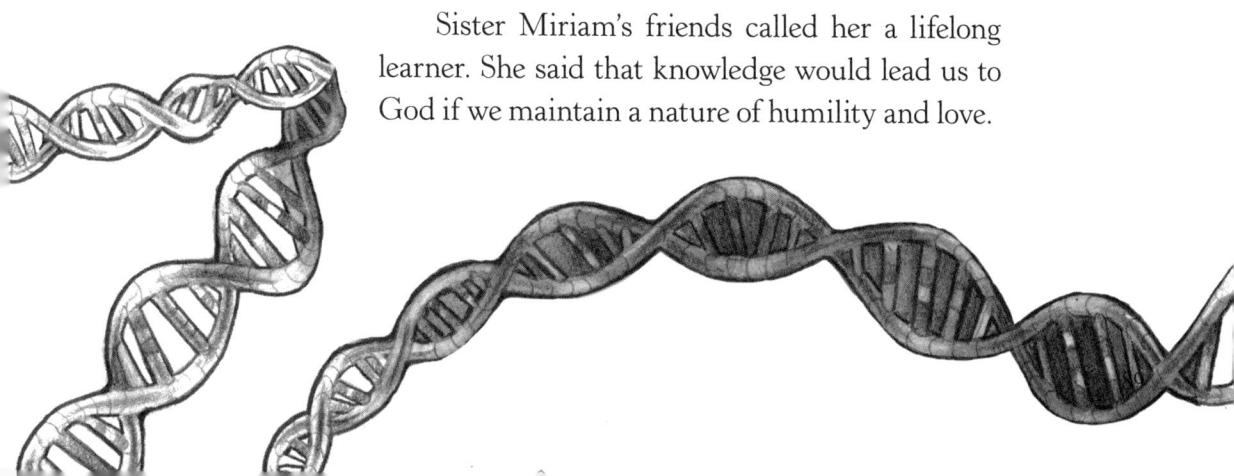

Sister Miriam's friends called her a lifelong learner. She said that knowledge would lead us to God if we maintain a nature of humility and love.

Just as the priest can touch Jesus

Saint Gianna Beretta Molla

Patron of Doctors, Mothers, and Unborn Children

(October 4, 1922–April 28, 1962)

Gianna was born in Italy as one of thirteen children. Her parents taught her the importance of faith and education.

When she was a teenager, Gianna promised Jesus that she would serve him for the rest of her life. She planned on doing this by taking care of sick people. She studied surgery at the University of Milan and then in Pavia, where she received her medical degree.

Gianna loved children, so she continued to study and became a **pediatrician**, a doctor who helps children. She opened her own clinic and cared for her young patients.

Gianna knew that people needed more than just medical care. Their souls needed care too! Since her teenage years she had been a member of Catholic Action and the Saint Vincent de Paul Society. She continued to serve others' spiritual needs through these groups.

so do we touch Jesus in the bodies of patients

Meanwhile Gianna was also thinking about marriage and family life. She met a Catholic businessman named Pietro Molla. He volunteered his time to help the needy and also loved God. Pietro and Gianna soon fell in love. Gianna wanted to marry Pietro, but was concerned. She knew that a good marriage would take time and effort. Could she marry Pietro and keep her promise of serving the sick? She prayed about this and concluded that if God was calling her to marriage, he would also help her still be a good doctor.

Gianna and Pietro got married in 1955. They prayed the Rosary together daily and looked forward to having a family.

Between 1956 and 1959, Gianna welcomed three beautiful children into the world. Then, she and Pietro experienced two miscarriages—when a pregnancy ends before the baby is ready to be born. In 1961, Gianna was expecting again, but this time a serious problem occurred. Gianna developed a dangerous fibroid tumor. The tumor threatened her life and the life of her unborn baby.

Gianna had to make a choice. She could have a hysterectomy—surgery that would remove her uterus (where the baby grows)—or she could have a surgery to remove only the tumor. A hysterectomy would end the life of her baby. But if Gianna had only the tumor removed, her own life could still be at risk. The Catholic Church teaches that purposely ending the life of an unborn baby is very wrong. However, if a hysterectomy was done in order to remove all traces of the cancer, it would not be a sin, even if it unintentionally caused the death of the unborn baby. Gianna chose to protect the life of her baby. She decided to have only the tumor removed, despite the risks to herself. She told her doctors, "If you must decide between me and the child, do not hesitate: choose the child—I insist on it." The birth of her child, Gianna Emanuela, was the result of this selfless choice. After the baby was born, Gianna was very sick due to complications after childbirth. She suffered in pain as she said,

"Jesus, I love you!" again and again. After one short week with her new baby, she passed away at the age of 39.

Gianna's promise to serve the sick helped many people. At least one doctor today continues to serve as a direct result of Gianna's heroism—Dr. Gianna Emanuela, Gianna's own daughter whose life she saved!

In 1994, Saint Pope John Paul II beatified Gianna during the Year of the Family. Gianna's husband and children attended the event. In 2004, she was named a saint. She is considered a patron of medical professionals. Her story of love and sacrifice inspires countless doctors everywhere. Today, many hospitals and clinics around the world bear her name.

Sister Mary Kenneth Keller

Pioneer in Computer Science
(December 17, 1913–January 10, 1985)

We live in a digital age. Most people have easy access to computers, smart phones, and tablets. It is hard to imagine a time before everyone had technology at their fingertips. Sister Mary Kenneth Keller lived in such a time, and it was not long ago.

In the 1950s, computers were rare, very expensive, and slow. They did not have color screens. The computers at that time were also huge! A single computer took up a whole room! They were so hard to use that only math experts could operate them. Thankfully, a smart nun who understood computers helped pave the way for everyone to use them.

the heart as for the... Lord.

Sister Mary Kenneth Keller was born in Cleveland, Ohio. At nineteen, she joined the Sisters of Charity of the Blessed Virgin Mary. This order of religious sisters thought education was very important and started a women's school called Clarke College. Mary made her first profession of religious vows in 1940, taking the name Sister Mary Kenneth. Later she attended DePaul University in Chicago, Illinois.

Sister Mary earned a master's degree in math and physics, but she wanted to continue learning. She was interested in computers and continued to learn more about them. In 1958, she was invited by the National Science Foundation to work in a computer workshop at Dartmouth College, in Hanover, New Hampshire. There was just one problem—Dartmouth was an all-male school. The rules did not allow a woman to enter its computer center. Thankfully, Dartmouth softened its rules and allowed Sister Mary to participate. She was the first woman to do so and she did it in a nun's habit!

Sister Mary played an important part in computer history. Her professors, John Kemeny and Tom Kurtz, said that computers needed to be simpler. It took a long time to do everything necessary to run a new program on a computer. Sister Mary saw how much computers could help improve education. But if they remained so complex, then most people would never be able to use them. With the help of her teachers, Sister Mary and the team developed a computer language called BASIC. The name is short for the "Beginners' All-Purpose Symbolic Instruction Code."

BASIC was a breakthrough. It made it easy for people to learn to type the commands. BASIC was soon taught in high schools and became the language used by many computers. Its use led to many computer programs, including early video games!

In the 1960s, Sister Mary studied at Purdue University in West Lafayette, Indiana and the University of Michigan in Ann Arbor,

Michigan. In 1965, she earned her PhD from the University of Wisconsin-Madison. She was the first woman to earn her doctorate in computer science!

After blazing a trail for women, Sister Mary returned to Clarke College to teach. She became a professor of computer science. She helped other women learn computers and spoke of the value that computers have in education. She founded a computer department and led it for twenty years.

Sister Mary wrote four books about computer science. She lived her life in a way that brought faith and a passion for education together.

Clarke College changed its name and is now a coeducational institute known as Clarke University in Dubuque, Iowa. There, the computer center and a major scholarship are both named after Sister Mary.

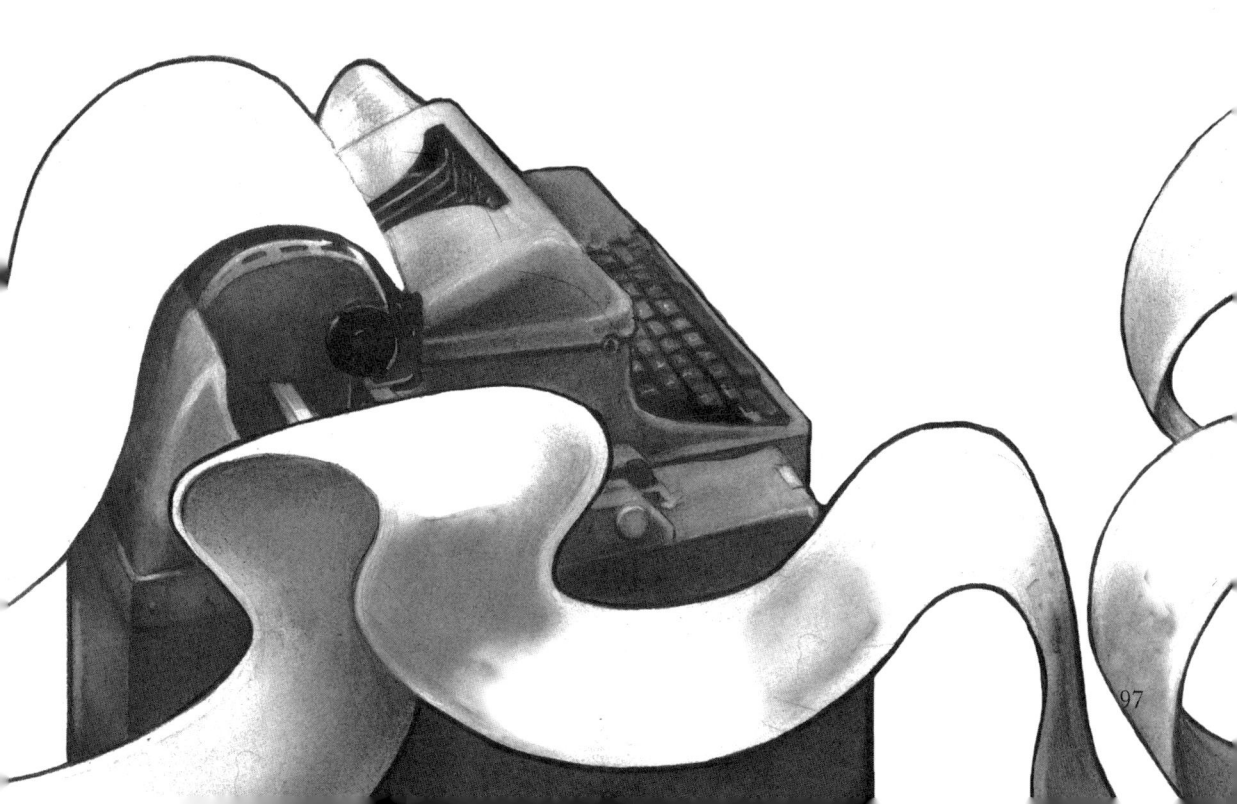

Jérôme Lejeune

Pediatrician, Geneticist, Servant of God
(June 13, 1926—April 3, 1994)

For every seven hundred babies born in the United States, one of them will likely have Down syndrome. The condition causes people to have a unique face, poor muscle tone, heart problems, and intellectual challenges. For many years, people believed wrongly that Down syndrome was passed down from parents. With this misunderstanding, scientists were unable to figure out what caused the condition. Thankfully, a Catholic doctor made a discovery that has helped scientists understand Down syndrome better.

Doctor Jérôme Lejeune was born in Paris, France. He had wanted to become a doctor ever since he was young. Toward the end of World War II, he studied medicine and developed a special connection with children who had Down syndrome. He called these children his "dear little ones." He decided to help them in a special way.

EACH OF US HAS TO FACE THE CHALLENGE OF DEALING WITH DIFFICULT SITUATIONS

AND I BELIEVE OUR RESPONSE

MUST BE GUIDED BY

HUMILITY AND COMPASSION

In 1958, a medical scientist named Marthe Gautier was looking at the heart cells of people who had Down syndrome in a microscope. She found something unusual, but her microscope was not powerful enough to see it well. Jérôme offered to take a look and used equipment to photograph the cells. By studying this abnormality, he found out that Down syndrome was caused by an extra copy of a person's twenty-first **chromosome**. The Latin word "trisomy" can mean three of something. Since Down syndrome presents three parts to the twenty-first chromosome instead of two, Down syndrome is sometimes called trisomy 21. The discovery meant that the condition was not passed down from parents as people had once thought. In 1959, the French Academy of Sciences shared the discovery. The news opened the door for new studies on how chromosomes affect our bodies.

The young doctor was celebrated for the discovery. American President John F. Kennedy gave him an award. Jérôme became a leader of the French National Center for Scientific Research. He taught in Paris and led a team to study over thirty thousand cases related to chromosomes. Many people felt that Jérôme should receive the Nobel Prize.

Soon, doctors used the discovery to find out if an unborn child had Down syndrome. This allowed the mother to prepare to raise a special child with this condition. Sometimes, once a mother found out, she would choose to have an abortion, a procedure that ends the life of her unborn baby. This is against Catholic teaching because it violates the commandment, "You shall not kill." Every baby, even one that has not been born yet, is a person made in the image of God. Jérôme became very upset when he learned how some doctors misused his discovery.

As a Catholic, Jérôme knew that all people, including those with Down syndrome, are worthy of dignity and respect. He was moved by Jesus' words, ". . . Whatever you did for one of these least brothers of mine, you did for me" (Mt 25:40).

In 1969, Jérôme received the William Allan Memorial Award, the highest award in genetics. At the ceremony, Jérôme decided to give a speech that he knew would be unpopular. He reminded the crowd of scientists and doctors that medicine is for saving lives. He also talked about why deciding to abort an unborn child because he or she has Down syndrome is wrong. Jérôme asked doctors to work toward finding a cure for Down syndrome instead.

Many people reacted negatively to the speech. Jérôme knew that people would no longer think of him as a nominee for the Nobel Prize. Lawmakers, famous people, and scientists all distanced themselves from the once-celebrated doctor. People who supported his research refused to offer any more money. Vandals painted the words "Death to Lejeune" on walls in Paris. Jérôme was even verbally attacked in front of his wife and five children. When this happened, he would smile and say, "It is not for myself that I'm fighting."

Jérôme's goal to defend the lives of those with Down syndrome was not over. He found friends in the Catholic Church who supported his work. He became a close friend of Pope Saint John Paul II and continued to speak in support of his "dear little ones."

Years later, the pope asked Jérôme to lead the new Pontifical Academy for Life. At first he hesitated. He had developed cancer and was suffering. He was not sure if he was up to the task. However, the pope encouraged him and inspired Jérôme to take on this role. He vowed that he would die in action, serving the cause of life. After serving only a short time, Jérôme passed away. Two years after his death, the Jérôme Lejeune Foundation opened to continue his life's work. The Catholic Church considers Jérôme a Servant of God and is investigating his case for sainthood.

LET US BE PROTECTORS of CREATION PROTECTORS of ONE ANOTHER

Pope Francis

Environmentalist, Scientific Advocate
(December 17, 1936–)

Pope Francis was born Jorge Bergoglio in Argentina, to parents of Italian descent. He was the oldest of five siblings in a Catholic home. As a teenager, Jorge's friends noticed that he always thought of the needs of others. Jorge was a talented student and was interested in science. After high school, he went to a state college and studied chemistry. He worked hard and grew into a kind young man. He worked as a chemical technician in the food industry.

One day, Jorge walked by a church and felt drawn to go in. He went to confession and felt inspired to give his life to God and become a priest. This call from God meant that he had to end a romantic relationship. He also had to convince his mother that he was meant for ministry—and she was not happy about this idea!

Jorge joined the Jesuit order in 1958 and entered the seminary. The Jesuits have a long history of teaching science along with theology. By the time Jorge became a priest in 1969, his mother fully supported his choice. She even asked him for a blessing!

Father Jorge taught theology and paid special attention to the needs of the poor. In 1992, Jorge became a bishop. Six years later, he became an archbishop. In 2001, Pope Saint John Paul II named him a cardinal.

On March 13, 2013, the cardinals elected Jorge to serve as pope. He chose the name Francis, after Saint Francis of Assisi. The name had a lot of meaning for the new pope. Saint Francis was a humble man who tried hard to be holy and who cared for the poor and the environment.

Pope Francis noticed that some people wondered how the Bible could possibly be true when so many parts of it seemed to go against science. He reminded them that modern science does not do away with the need for God. After all, someone or something had to begin the formation of the universe. Catholicism teaches that God created the universe and holds it in existence. Even creatures that evolve still require a creator to make them exist. God may have used the process of evolution to form the human body. Humans also have a soul, which is created directly by God. If Catholics understand that God is always involved in the universe and in the creation of human beings, they do not have to choose between faith and science. They can embrace both.

In 2014, Pope Francis repeated that the theories of the Big Bang and **evolution** were compatible with the teaching of creation. Many news outlets reported that Pope Francis broke away from the Church's teaching about science. This was not true. Throughout history, Catholicism has supported scientific learning. Pope Francis was not the first one to say that. Pope Benedict XVI, Pope Saint John

Paul II, and Pope Pius XII all said that the theory of evolution does not contradict Catholic teaching.

The Catholic Church teaches that the Bible reveals the truth of God's love for creation and the human race. The Bible is a collection of many books. Some books contain stories that were told by early Jewish people. Some passages are historical, while other parts contain poetry and songs. Readers who think that the Bible is teaching science miss the bigger message—that God is the Creator of the universe, that he loves us, and that we should love him and one another.

Pope Francis did not stop by clarifying this teaching about faith and science. He built healthy relationships with the world's leading scientists, like Stephen Hawking (1942–2018). Hawking did not believe in God, but he was a member of the Papal Academy of Science. Hawking agreed with Pope Francis that scientists and people of faith should work together for the common good of people and the Earth.

In 2015, Pope Francis shared his letter, *Laudato Si' (Praise Be to You): On Care for our Common Home*. The title was inspired by Saint Francis of Assisi's poem, "Canticle of the Creatures," which praises God for his creation. The Pope's letter says that taking care of the poor means we must also take care of the Earth. It also says that people should work together to help the Earth by reducing the human causes of global warming. Pope Francis reminded readers that God will judge how people take care of the Earth. In 2016, Pope Francis declared taking care of creation as a new Catholic work of mercy.

Pope Francis reminds Catholics of their duty to use scientific knowledge to take care of the Earth and promote peace. He also proves that Christian and non-Christian scientists can work together to protect our common home.

> MY FAITH GIVES
> TO MY CURIOSITY
> THE UNIVERSE

Karin Öberg

Astrochemist, Professor

(August 27, 1982–)

In a desert of Chile that is nearly fifteen thousand feet above the sea exists some of the world's most advanced technology. It is the home of ALMA—the "Atacama Large Millimeter/submillimeter Array"—a powerful telescope that allows scientists to detect the chemicals around distant young stars and planets. ALMA has sixty-six antennas that aim toward the stars. Karin Öberg, an astrochemist and Catholic, uses ALMA to find answers to questions about how life began on our planet and whether it might exist elsewhere in our galaxy. For Karin, searching the skies is as much about understanding God as it is about understanding the stars.

Karin was born in a small town in Sweden. Her father was a chemist who taught her science before she could read. He gave her scientific toys and shared his love of the stars with her. In high school, Karin proved to be gifted at chemistry, but she was more interested in physics. The thought of going to college to study one and not the other left her feeling torn.

Karin went to the California Institute of Technology (Caltech) in Pasadena, California. She was delighted when she discovered that she could use both chemistry and physics in the field of **astrochemistry**—the study of molecules and their chemistry in space. After she earned a degree in chemistry she earned her doctorate in astronomy at Leiden University in the Netherlands. Karin worked hard and excelled in her studies. Jon Morse, **NASA**'s former director of astrophysics, has called Karin one of the best and brightest young astronomers in the world. She studied astrophysics at Harvard in Cambridge, Massachusetts. She became a professor of chemistry at the University of Virginia in Charlottesville, Virginia, and then returned to Harvard as a professor.

Aside from being supersmart, Karin is also a devoted Catholic. But she was not always this way. Karin was not raised Catholic and her home was not very religious. As a teen, Karin doubted if God was real.

However, some spiritual thoughts swirled in her mind. Karin believed that good and evil were real. She also believed in free will. These ideas challenged her thinking. Karin spoke with Christians who left an impression on her. She started to consider that God might be real after all!

When Karin was studying in Leiden, she read a book called *Mere Christianity* by C. S. Lewis. A short hour into reading it, Karin decided to become Christian. Soon she joined a church and met more thoughtful followers of Christ. Karin read *Orthodoxy* by G. K. Chesterton and became sure that the Catholic Church was the one true faith with authority. Soon after, she entered an **RCIA** program and became a Catholic.

Karin now leads the Öberg Astrochemistry Group at Harvard. Her team studies the chemical makeup of young stars to understand how planets form. They search the universe for clues that explain how water and other materials came to Earth. They also use advanced science to figure out how likely it is that planets have life on them. In 2015, the group made a major discovery of a complex molecule found on a disk that surrounded a new star.

For Karin, this exciting research is about more than understanding other galaxies. It is also about understanding the God who created them. Karin said, "Knowing that everything in the universe reflects God in one way or another makes it very exciting to turn our telescopes toward other stars and see planetary systems like our own around them. Studying how these other worlds came about reflects the glory and creativity of God in a very special way."

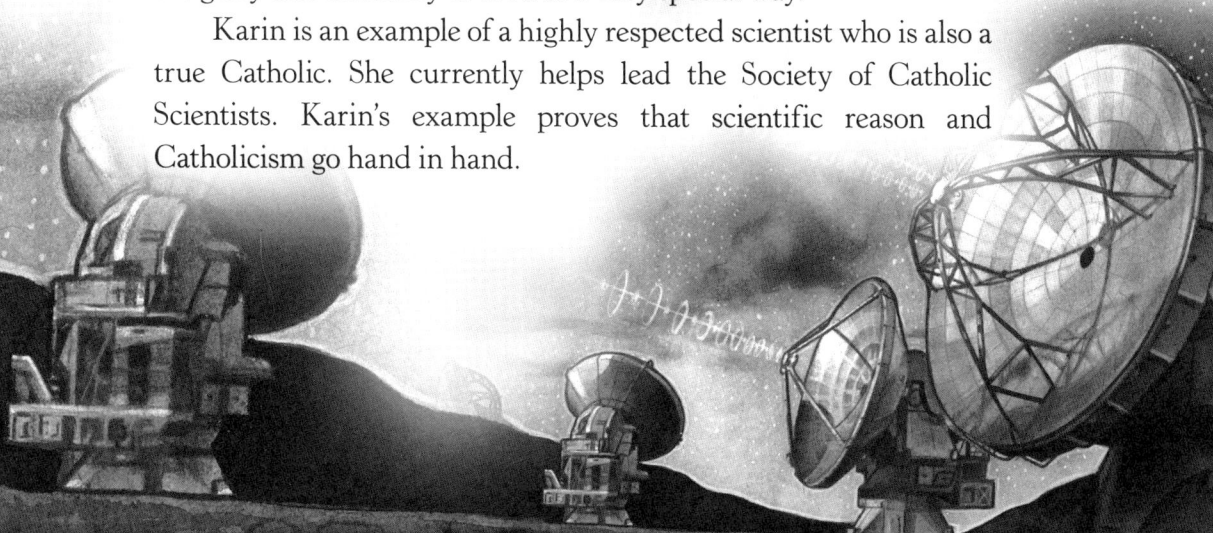

Karin is an example of a highly respected scientist who is also a true Catholic. She currently helps lead the Society of Catholic Scientists. Karin's example proves that scientific reason and Catholicism go hand in hand.

Glossary

abbess a woman who is a leader of a group of nuns in an abbey or monastery

abbot the leader of an abbey where monks live, work, and pray

anatomist a scientist who studies the human body

anatomy the study of the human body

anthrax a dangerous disease caused by bacteria that affects the skin and lungs

archeologist a person who studies prehistory and looks at artifacts

arsenic a poisonous chemical that can be used in glassmaking or preserving wood

astrochemistry the study of molecules and their reactions to radiation in space

astronomy the study of space and the physical properties of the universe

astrophysics the study of stars and objects in space in relation to physics

atheist a person who does not believe in God

bacteriology the study of bacteria

botany the study of plants

Bronze Age a prehistoric time when weapons and tools were made out of bronze

calculus math that helps us understand and predict changes

canonization the process of officially declaring someone a saint in the Catholic Church

catechist a person who shares the Catholic faith with others, by teaching and personal witness. In remote missionary areas, the catechist may lead prayer and perform Baptisms and weddings in the absence of a priest

chemistry the science of identifying chemicals and how they interact and change

cholera a dangerous disease caused by bacteria that affects the small intestine

chromosome a molecule that contains genetic information

corona the outermost part of a star's atmosphere

cycloid a special curve that is made when a circle is rolled across a straight line

DNA deoxyribonucleic acid, part of a chromosome that contains genetic information

doctor of the Church a Catholic saint whose teaching and writing are considered worthy of guiding the faithful throughout time

eclipse when a source of light is blocked by something that gets between it and the viewer

genetics the study of genes and the traits that are passed down from ancestors

harmonics sound tones that vibrate at a specific wave interval above another tone

heliocentric a way to describe that the sun, and not the Earth, is at the center of our solar system

horticulture the practice of keeping a garden

hymenoptera a group of insects that includes ants, wasps, and bees

insulin a chemical that controls the amount of sugar in blood

Julian calendar a slightly incorrect calendar that replaced the Roman calendar under the authority of Julius Caesar

KBr disk method a way of preparing samples for observation with a spectroscope

meningitis a dangerous infection that causes the brain and parts of the spinal cord to swell

microbiology the science of germs and microbes

NASA National Aeronautics and Space Administration, America's federal space agency dedicated to science and technology

pasteurization a process named after Louis Pasteur that involves heating liquids and then quickly cooling them to kill germs

pathology the study of diseases, especially their causes and effects

pediatrician a doctor who specifically focuses on treating children

pharmacy the science of making medical drugs

philosophy the study of reality, the nature of truth, and how we know things

physiology the study of the normal functioning of the parts of the human body

pitch the highness or lowness of a sound tone

Principle of Superposition the idea that layers of the Earth are stacked on top of one another over very long periods of time

prime number a whole number greater than one that only has one and itself as factors

prioress a woman who is a leader of a group of nuns

Punnett square a graphical way of figuring out the possible combinations of inherited traits

RCIA Rite of Christian Initiation for Adults, a program that allows adults to learn more about and prepare to join the Catholic Church

rabies a deadly disease spread by the spit of certain animals

refract to break up or bend light by changing its direction, often through a prism

Saint Vincent de Paul Society a worldwide organization of Catholic men and women who serve Christ by serving the poor and suffering. Many parishes have Saint Vincent de Paul Society groups

Shinto an ancient Japanese religion that emphasizes rituals and the honoring of many spirits

silver nitrate a chemical compound that can be used as an antiseptic

solar system the grouping of planets and moons that circle around a star

spectroscope a tool that measures light waves to see molecules or chemicals

stethoscope a simple device that allows doctors to listen to sounds coming from inside the body

Stone Age a period of prehistory during which simple tools were made out of stone

strata layers of rocks in the ground

theory of evolution a theory about how species change over time

tropical year 365.24219 days, the actual length of time it takes for the Earth to circle the sun

tuberculosis a contagious disease that affects the lungs and can cause a person to have a fever

ultraviolet light a type of light that is not visible to the human eye

vaccine a substance that helps a person develop immunity and protection from diseases

X-ray a method of using electromagnetic radiation to get a picture of the inside of the body

To learn more about these brilliant men and women, check out the "For Further Reading" list at https://paulinestore.com/brilliant-reading

Jaclyn Warren (illustrator) grew up in Louisiana where she fostered a deep love for art, Cajun culture, and Catholicism. She studied drawing and painting at the Savannah College of Art and Design and earned her master's degree in Art Therapy at Florida State University.

David Michael Warren (author) grew up searching for great stories in comic books, movies, church sermons, and anywhere else he could find them. When he studied film at the Savannah College of Art and Design, he met Jaclyn, heard the story of Catholicism, and converted to the faith.

Today, Jaclyn loves to spend time with her family and find ways to use art to help others, and David lives out his love of stories by writing and making movies. Together they live in beautiful Covington, Louisiana, with their children.

Photo credit: Heather Burbrink

Who are the Daughters of St. Paul?

We are Catholic sisters with a mission. Our task is to bring the love of Jesus to everyone like Saint Paul did. You can find us in over 50 countries. Our founder, Blessed James Alberione, showed us how to reach out to the world through the media. That's why we publish books, make movies and apps, record music, broadcast on radio, perform concerts, help people at our bookstores, visit parishes, use social media and the Internet, and pray for all of you.

smile
God loves you